HEROIN ADDICTION
IN BRITAIN

Horace Freeland Judson

HEROIN ADDICTION
IN BRITAIN
What Americans Can Learn
from the English Experience

HARCOURT BRACE JOVANOVICH
NEW YORK AND LONDON

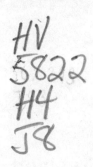

Printed in the United States of America

Most of the material in this book appeared originally in *The New Yorker,* in slightly different form.

Library of Congress Cataloging in Publication Data

Judson, Horace Freeland.
Heroin addiction in Britain.

Includes bibliographical references.
1. Heroin habit. 2. Drug abuse—Great Britain.
3. Drug abuse—Treatment—Great Britain. I. Title.
HV5822.H4J8   362.2′93′0942   74-11236
ISBN 0-15-140098-9

First edition

B C D E

About the ultimate aspects of the drug problem, America and Britain are experiencing absolutely identical concerns. The fundamentals are common: it is only when those fundamentals are overlaid by the particular circumstances of a national scene that we are falsely led to believe that our two nations face an entirely different set of dilemmas. For instance, we have in common the need to delineate what we believe to be the causes of our drug problems, for those beliefs potently determine our policies: we must share therefore a vital concern to identify the nature and validity of causal assumptions. America and Britain may respond variously to this or that type of drug-using individual, but we both have the problem of determining how best to respond to the individual, and we share a confusion in often not knowing whether to respond to him as sick or as bad. We may sometimes seem to have different ideas as to the degree to which the state should in this area curtail the individual's liberty: we are identically concerned with the fundamental question of liberty.

—Griffith Edwards, addressing the Anglo-American Conference on Drug Abuse, sponsored by the Royal Society of Medicine, in London, 15–18 April 1973

Contents

Preface

Social policies find few laboratories, even metaphorically, to test them: when a major social problem has been attacked in two countries from two almost opposite approaches—as the problem of narcotics addiction has been attacked in Great Britain and the United States—a comparison of the results ought to be instructive. Yet until now the facts about narcotics addiction and narcotics policy in Great Britain have been hard to come by; they have often been misreported, still more often distorted or misunderstood. In London, in the late 1960s, where I was working as a correspondent, I frequently read American reports about the British epidemic of heroin addiction and repeatedly found myself throwing down the newspaper or magazine in annoyance at what seemed to be simple, fundamental, chronic errors of fact. The irritation would not heal. Eventually, I proposed to write an article of perhaps ten thousand words to set the facts straight. Of course, the facts were less simple than I had thought, and their consequences more ambiguous; and it soon turned out that people's attitudes are the most fundamental facts of all about drug addiction and the policies that purport to deal with it. Ambiguities and attitudes, though, sometimes resist direct statement and must be allowed to convey themselves. The article, when it ran in *The New Yorker* in September and October 1973, was nearly four times the length originally planned. It has grown by a third again to book form: there was more to be said about the ways that British policy evolved in the 1920s and after the Second World War; some new research into addiction had been completed in England; and I was ready to press further, in a new part 3, the lessons that Americans can and cannot draw from the British experience. Drug addiction is a subject so raddled with misinformation that I have provided notes on sources, except for a few things learned from men who asked not to be quoted by name; it is pleasant to demonstrate that a report of this informal kind can be reasonably rigorous, but the most gratifying assurance of accuracy came from the director of a drug-addiction clinic in London who said that he asks new members of his staff to read the article as an introduction to their work. I remain unable to know whether I have changed any attitudes but my own or reached any but the most local conclusions; I'm confident at least that my original aim is satisfied, in that the elementary facts about narcotics addiction and narcotics policy in Great Britain have been mustered, and will be found to be present and correct.

A man to whom I had listened carefully while preparing this book contented himself after he had read the magazine version with observing, "In matters of science or scholarship I've always believed, of course, that ideas are common property from the moment one mutters them in one's bath." Perhaps, indeed, it's pretentious for an exercise in journalism to dress itself in charts and footnotes and grandfather's tail coat and play at being grown up into that world of science and scholarship; but one piece of the apparatus I welcome—this chance to thank the people to whom I tried to listen carefully, and whose ideas have therefore found their way in here. My debt to Griffith Edwards will be evident to every reader; though I spent too little time with him, and spent that time so engrossed that I came away with only a few pages of scribbled key words, almost everything he said to me about drug addiction appears somewhere within—supposing, that is, that I got it right. I owe a similar debt to Martin Mitcheson and Margaret Tripp. In New York, Graham Finney and Thomas Bryant told me who in England not to miss and what questions not to forget. In London, C. G. Jeffery and H. B. Spear, of the Drugs Branch of the Home Office, gave hours of time and yards of the knowledge they uniquely possess. And then so many people let me interrupt their work, offering so much information beyond what is attributed to them in the text, that there's no fair way to single out the contribution of each. I am very grateful, for interviews in England, to Thomas Bewley, Philip Connell, Max Glatt, Edward David Hill, Ian Pierce James, John Mack, Susan Norvill, Gisela Brigitte Oppenheim, and James Willis, all at addiction-treatment clinics, and to those of their clients who also talked with me; and to Don Aitken, of Release, Peter A. L. Chapple, of the National Addiction and Research Institute, Cicely Saunders, of St. Christopher's Hospice, Roy Jenkins, Home Secretary in 1968 and now again, Peter Beedle, at the Home Office, Dennis Cahal, Ian Jewesbury, Alan Sippert, and E. R. Bransby, all at the Department of Health and Social Security, Commander Robert Huntley, of the Metropolitan Police, David Hawks and Colin Roberts, at the Addiction Research Unit of the Institute of Psychiatry, Jasper Woodcock, of the Institute for the Study of Drug Dependence, and Jim Zacune, of North Staffordshire Polytechnic; and for interviews in the United States, I want to thank Elmer

xii   *Preface*

Gardner, Ray Godfrey, John Kramer, Robert Newman, Charles Rangel, and James E. Wesley. Three other Americans, whom I first met in England and sought out again in the United States, made me understand what I had learned, and for that necessary service I salute Richard Blum, Daniel X. Freedman, and Norman Zinberg. William Shawn gave editorial support and criticism generously; I hope I learned something of his fastidious courtesy to the reader. I also want to thank, for information or good counsel, Irving Benjamin, Caroline Coon, C. P. Crow, Risa Dickstein, Sir Harry Greenfield, G. G. Halliday, Kenneth Leech, Andrew Schaffer, Maria Squerciati, Herbert Sturz, and the staffs of the London Library, the medical library at the New York Academy of Medicine, the Institute for the Study of Drug Dependence, and the Cambridge University Medical Library. Some of those I've mentioned also read part or all of the manuscript, at one stage or another, and made essential corrections. So, too, did Helga Veblen, in the checking department of *The New Yorker*, who reinterviewed as many of my informants as she could reach, and found a dozen other authorities as well—whom I also thank, and in particular David Musto, who spent hours on the telephone, combing out factual snarls in the account of the early history of narcotics control in the United States. Dr. Veblen was hampered by the fact that many people I had talked to were thousands of miles away, so that, against her better judgment, she was obliged to pencil in, next to paragraph after paragraph of her galley proofs, the reluctant notation "O.A."—meaning, she said, that the responsibility for error was on the author. As, of course, for every paragraph, it is.

Meldreth, Cambridgeshire
March 1974

HEROIN ADDICTION
IN BRITAIN

1

The Past: Heroin Maintenance and the Epidemic of Addiction in England, to 1968

My first encounter and only personal experience with heroin took place in 1966, when I was living in London. What everybody knows about the British and heroin is that they supply it on prescription to heroin addicts. But my first sight of the drug seemed to have nothing to do with addicts. My elder daughter, then seven, had caught a cold and developed a hacking cough. The doctor listened at her bedside—English doctors still sometimes call at bedsides—and then wrote out a prescription for cough medicine. As we left together, I on my way to the pharmacist's, I glanced at what he had written, and disentangled the words "elixir diamorphinae."

"Isn't that heroin?"

My tone made the doctor laugh. "You've got the American horror of it," he said. (I certainly had.) "Really, the amount is homeopathic—well, almost. And it's the best thing in the world for a bad cough, heroin."

The pharmacist at the corner filled the prescription while I waited, and without so much as giving me a hard look. The

medicine seemed to do the trick: my daughter stopped cough-
ing. Later that winter, I had an irritating night-time cough
myself. There was still some syrup at the bottom of the bottle.
I swallowed a spoonful. Homeopathic dose or not, it killed
the tickle.

Cough medicine was, in fact, heroin's first general therapeutic use. The stuff was discovered in 1874—seventy years
after the original isolation of morphine from opium—when the
London chemist C. R. Alder Wright, starting an exhaustive
catalogue of the actions of organically derived acids on morphine, cooked some morphine with acetic anhydride, a pungent
liquid closely related to the familiar acetic acid that gives
vinegar its zest. Heroin was christened in 1898 by Heinrich
Dreser, chief pharmacologist at the Elberfeld Farbenfabrik of
Friedrich Bayer & Company, in a paper he read to the seven-
tieth Congress of German Naturalists and Physicians, in Düsseldorf. (A year later, Dreser coined for Bayer another
memorable name—"aspirin.") He announced to the congress
in Düsseldorf that tests of heroin on animals in his laboratory
—and, at his direction, on sixty unsuspecting patients in the
dyeworks' own hospital—demonstrated that the new narcotic
was sovereign for cough, catarrh, bronchitis, emphysema, tuberculosis, and asthma. It was free of the undesirable side
effects of morphine, such as nausea, vomiting, constipation,
and loss of appetite. Then, too, he reported, patients said great
things about the drug: *"Herr Doktor, die Pulver, die Sie mir
gaben*—that powder you gave me, doctor, it worked so well,
right away when I took it I felt relief"—the whining supplica-
tion echoes back, surely, to the first apothecary with a new
drug to pluck the sleeve of Hippocrates himself, the promise
that patients will be eased and full of thanks. Doctors, after
all, are gratified very deeply, close to the root of their being as
doctors, by certain kinds of response that drugs can elicit from

patients. Beyond others, the opiates—especially heroin—are capable of tangling up a doctor's motives. This unpleasant fact intrudes again and again in the control of drug addiction.

In Dreser's list of heroin's heroic properties, he mentioned in passing that it seemed not to be habit-forming. That error, of course, has made the introduction of heroin one of the great cautionary tales of medicine, not to be equaled until another German drugmaker launched another analgesic into the vocabulary—thalidomide. Dreser published his report in Germany in the fall of 1898; in November, his talk was noted by *The Journal of the American Medical Association;* within weeks, other clinicians were confirming heroin's efficacy in the treatment of cough. In December, *The Lancet,* the British journal of clinical medicine, called for English tests and noted that heroin was already being distributed by the London agency for Bayer, 19 St. Dunstan's-Hill, E.C.

Heroin is lawful today, for at least some medical uses, in nine of the 188 countries and territories whose requirements for opiates and cocaine are compiled and published every year by the International Narcotics Control Board, an organ of the United Nations, in Geneva. (Only the People's Republic of China is unreported.) Most of the heroin legally manufactured in the world is made the same way Wright first made it in London in 1874. Given the crude morphine, to synthesize heroin takes far less apparatus, time, and chemical experience than, say, to distill a drinkable whiskey. The morphine molecule is a compact linkage of three carbon rings, crocheted together by a fourth loop containing a nitrogen atom. Even some vitamins are chemically more complex. Heroin is exactly like morphine except that from each of two of the carbon rings there dangles a short chain of atoms taken on from the acetic anhydride. Pure heroin is a white powder almost insoluble in water. Exposed to air, it begins losing acetyl groups, smelling vinegary, and turning pink. Heroin does not appear in *The United States Pharmacopeia*. The more stable salt of the stuff is listed in *The United States Dispensatory*, a handbook for pharmacists, as "diacetylmorphine hydrochloride," and in the *British Pharmacopoeia* as "diamorphine hydrochloride." This is an odorless, almost white crystalline substance with a bitter taste. It dissolves readily in water. In most of the countries where heroin is still legal, the amounts permitted are small: 250 grams in the Netherlands in 1974, for example, 100 grams in West Germany, and the same in Ireland, down to 10 grams in Poland, 9 grams in Bahrain, 7 grams in New Zealand. Great Britain licensed the production of 80 kilograms in 1974 (10 kilos less than the previous year), out of the total world requirement of 95 kilos 606 grams. That entire lawful British supply of diamorphine is manufactured by a Scottish firm, Macfarlan Smith, Ltd. (cable address "Morphine"), of Edinburgh. Starting with imported opium, and under extreme security precautions—even the firm's wall calendar, with a dreamy painting of *Papaver somniferum*, the opium poppy, is restricted in distribution—this factory produces a variety of alkaloids. The 80 kilos of heroin would have a street value in the United States of over fifty million dollars. It is unlikely that Macfarlan Smith makes enough profit on its heroin to be worth the trouble. None of it is exported. Thirty-five kilos will be converted into a different drug, nalorphine, which is a narcotic antagonist. (Injected, it counteracts any morphine or heroin in an addict's body, throwing him quickly into withdrawal.) The 45 kilos remaining for consumption as diamorphine hydrochloride may not all be used. In fact, the legal consumption of heroin in Britain in 1972 was down nearly a third from its peak in 1968. Lawful heroin in Britain is most commonly seen in white tablets about the size of saccharin tablets, each containing ten milligrams, one-sixth of a grain.

The pills cost the National Health Service two and a quarter cents each. To get a prescription filled (whatever the drug or dose) costs a patient the equivalent of fifty cents.

How heroin or any other opiate works on the central nervous system is not fully understood. Neurobiologists propose that each molecule of narcotic fits exactly, key in lock, into a receptor on the outer membrane of a nerve cell, and thus changes the nerve's response to the normal stimulating chemicals produced and transmitted by other nerve cells nearby. If the nerve, to compensate, grows more receptors, or if it varies its utilization of the normal chemicals received from its neighbors, that would explain why narcotic doses must be increased to achieve the same pain relief or the same pleasure. Pharmacologists at Johns Hopkins University demonstrated recently that molecules of morphine or methadone do attach themselves to specific types of cells within the brain. More recently still, Avram Goldstein and colleagues at Stanford have announced that they have extracted and partially purified, from brain cells of mice, receptor molecules that interact specifically with opiates. The day is surely not far off when the structure of the receptors will be known and the mechanism of their response to opiates will be worked out atom by atom; yet until then such models remain no more than highly educated metaphors. But the fact of heroin's profound effect on the nerves is of course unquestionable. English doctors, speaking from clinical experience with heroin, call it the most potent analgesic they know, and a powerful tranquilizer. The effects are subjective and hard to measure; heroin and morphine differ more in some effects than in others; but even though the two are so similar in structure, heroin is estimated to be two to six times as strong. Despite these serviceable qualities, importation and manufacture of heroin are forbidden in America, its use for any purpose anathematized. Most American doctors are convinced, largely by hearsay, that heroin is too quickly addictive, and the euphoria it can produce too strongly, even sinfully pleasurable to be safe. Their reference books tell them that better drugs are available for every medical use.

English doctors disagree. Even those who are alarmed about the spread of addiction in their country believe that their American colleagues are stubbornly unprofessional to condone a ban on heroin. They discern at least seven medical uses for it. Among these, they don't defend heroin for coughs with any great conviction. Codeine will really do as well. Soon after taking my spoonful of heroin cough syrup, though, I met a magnificent Englishwoman, Cicely Saunders, whose vocation is the care of the dying. Many of her patients, of course, suffer from cancer. Dr. Saunders has become expert in the control of pain, and also in the control of less obvious causes of extreme distress, such as nausea and the shortness of breath that leads to the sensation of air hunger. She said, and most of her English colleagues agree, that heroin is often the best drug for terminal cancer patients, though she sometimes supplements it with gin. Like morphine, heroin not only blunts the panic of air hunger but can even lessen the fact of it, reducing acute pulmonary edema. Heroin is less likely than morphine to induce nausea. It relieves pain, but more than that, it is uniquely powerful in distancing the patient from what pain he still feels, and from his anxieties. For such patients, addiction is almost inevitable, and almost irrelevant. Yet Dr. Saunders said that their heroin dosages can be well controlled for many months; she will wake patients in the middle of the night to give them heroin so that the pain, and the necessary dose, never get out of control. Intense pain in heart attack is also treated with heroin—again because it freezes anxiety so effectively, as well as pain, and because it is less likely to nauseate. For coronary thrombosis, the need is transitory and addiction unlikely; this use of heroin is increasing. Some English surgeons consider heroin preferable to all other analgesics the night after an abdominal operation. An eminent physician, Henry G. Miller, vice-chancellor of the University of Newcastle upon Tyne, wrote in 1973 that heroin "is an unequalled and irreplaceable remedy for the intense paroxysmal pain that sometimes follows an attack of shingles in the elderly patient, but in many years of its regular prescription I have yet to encounter the patient who failed to return the remaining tablets after the pain had—as it practically always does—finally subsided." Dr. Miller also noted, testily and more generally, that "an unholy combination of neurotic fear of addiction with the traditional Christian glorification of suffering leads a minority of physicians to practice unjustifiable parsimony in the dispensation of pain-relieving drugs (just to be on the safe side, most doctor-patients take their favorite analgesics into hospital in their sponge-bags, together with their favorite sleeping tablets)."

In a conversation with Gisela Oppenheim, a psychiatrist, who runs the drug-addiction treatment center at Charing Cross Hospital, in London, I was told of still another use for heroin in medical crises. As it happens, Dr. Oppenheim has strong views against giving addicts heroin; it was these views I had come to hear. She said she had not prescribed heroin for a new addict patient in three years. Then did she think heroin should be banned in England, as it is in the United States? "Oh, no," she said. "I think heroin is a very useful drug. I worked once in a plastic-surgery ward. We were treating children who had been severely burned. Give them morphine and they might vomit all over. Give them a small shot of heroin and they'd calm down, become less tense—more able to face the visits to the operating theater for dressings. I would hate to see heroin abolished."

Everywhere else in the world, "the British approach to heroin" signifies the other principal medical use the drug is put to: legal, cheap, pure heroin for heroin addicts through government clinics. Before 1968, an addict got his prescriptions for heroin from any general practitioner willing to take him on as a patient. The clinics, where addicts must now come for their prescriptions, were set up only after turbulent debate, touched off by a small but explosive outbreak of new cases of heroin addiction, particularly among adolescents. Inevitably, the clinics are the dominant feature of the British approach as seen from abroad, and the focus of the arguments that continue about heroin at home. Yet in British terms the clinics for addicts and the rules that govern them are a unique limitation of the doctor's powers: it is still true today that—for any patient who is not an addict—any physician practicing in the United Kingdom can write a prescription for heroin and a pharmacist will fill it under the same controls that govern the use of any other strong narcotic. Of the many contrasts between British and American handling of addiction, heroin's place in ordinary British medical practice is perhaps the most arresting.

Ripped from its English context, as it almost always is, the idea of lawful heroin for addicts provokes either advocacy or passionate rejection among Americans who have to deal with the American heroin epidemic. Seen from London in 1968, one exasperating result of the switch from general practitioners' prescriptions to drug clinics was the smug American judgment that the British approach to controlling heroin addiction had proved a failure. At least in the short run the judgment was wrong. So in the past few years American doctors and bureaucrats have streamed over to visit the clinics. More and more often, the visitors have been telling their hosts that the idea of trying out legal heroin for addicts—"you know, the British system"—has acquired political standing in the United States. A current version of that idea is to experiment with cheap legal heroin as a "treatment lure" (the ugly phrase characterized a proposal made in 1972 by the Vera Institute of Justice, a small New York City foundation that specializes in criminology) to bring addicts in for cure who have failed in other programs. Implicit in all such proposals, and the reason for their political volatility, is the belief that to legalize heroin for addicts more than experimentally would mean that those who can't or won't give up the drug will at least give up the black market and crime.

It soon becomes evident to Americans investigating addiction in England—for one thing, their hosts tell them—that the British really have no single, exportable solution. The government counted 1,619 narcotics addicts in Britain at the end of 1972, the latest figure. In Washington, the Bureau of Narcotics and Dangerous Drugs estimated in January 1973 that there were 626,000 heroin addicts in the United States, while in New York City alone local officials reckon that there may be a quarter of a million heroin users—or more; they confess they do not know—of whom, more certainly, 150,000 are true addicts. The difference between the British and the American figures translates into huge differences in cost, in the ways addicts interact with each other and with the rest of society, in the organization of medical manpower, in administrative controls, in *ethical* controls. The difference in scale is so vast— two orders of magnitude, as a physicist would put it—that it all but overwhelms other comparisons and reasonable discussion. That said, it remains true that the British are the only people with a coherent experience of epidemic drug addiction to have dealt with heroin under policies markedly different from those that have long prevailed in the United States. And, whether by policy or by luck (their most thoughtful observers are not sure which), they have so far been successful in containing addiction.

The Maudsley Hospital, a tumble of brown and gray buildings lapped by motor traffic in London south of the Thames, is England's foremost psychiatric hospital for research and teaching. The Addiction Research Unit occupies a two-story prefabricated box in a parking lot at the Maudsley. Griffith Edwards, director of the unit, is a tall, stooped Welshman, ironically courteous to his American visitors—and that old-fashioned delight, a physician with a scholar's sense of the history of his subject. In a conversation a while ago over an institutional lunch—a pale, English institutional lunch of poached fresh fish fillets, broad beans, and stewed gooseberries with custard sauce—Dr. Edwards said, "One wonders how far the differences between the British and American drug problems are really the consequences of social policies. *Ab initio,* just how much addiction was there in the U.S. and the U.K. in the early '20s, when the very basic differences in approach between the two countries began to take shape? Did the American problem originate much earlier, with the importation of Chinese labor, and so on? Was the heroin problem already a ghetto problem in 1912? Or did it have its origin in the Harrison Narcotics Act of 1914, as people say? The relation between a drug and a community can be very unstable—*our* problem with heroin, barbiturates, and amphetamines may, possibly, be unstable right now. But take the British and alcohol, or India and cannabis—sometimes the relationship is not at all easy to change."

A formula in vogue just now in the United States has it that

Americans chose almost from the beginning to deal with heroin addiction by "the enforcement model," while the British chose "the medical model." Modelmakers oversimplify. Both the policeman and the physician have been heard from repeatedly in England, as in the United States. But from the first, the policeman in the United States has been urged on by the missionary—an alliance which has given American narcotics enforcement its characteristic fervor, and which the English have always viewed with distaste. Certainly, and without oversimplification, the international campaign to police the traffic in narcotics has always been led by the United States. The campaign began in the first years of the century, after the Spanish-American War, when the United States emerged as a Pacific power, took control of the Philippines, and discovered the opium trade in those islands and elsewhere in the Far East, especially China. The reaction of American reformers was to persuade Theodore Roosevelt to call for a conference of all nations with interests in the Far East, and then—as a demonstration of American sincerity at the conference—to push through Congress the first federal law limiting the use of narcotics, a simple ban on the importation of opium for smoking, approved in February 1909. The Shanghai Opium Commission convened that same month. Its chairman was the chief of the American delegation, Charles Henry Brent, who had been the first Episcopal bishop of the Philippines. The resolutions of the commission were mild, and dealt for the most part with the suppression of opium smoking and the commerce in opium; one resolution, introduced by the British and unanimously agreed to, said that governments ought to take strong measures to control morphine and other derivatives. The Shanghai Opium Commission was followed, again at American insistence, by the first International Conference on Opium, for which delegations from twelve countries met at

The Hague at the end of 1911; Bishop Brent again presided. The conference produced the Hague Opium Convention. Chapter Three of the convention required the nations to control morphine, heroin, any new derivatives that proved dangerous, and cocaine. The United States Senate ratified the convention by the end of 1913, and the Congress was then considering the Harrison Narcotics Bill, but other nations were slower to put the convention into effect. Then the war intervened. However, the Hague Opium Convention has been the basis for international control of narcotics; it was accepted by the British, and nearly everybody else, after it was wrapped into the Treaty of Versailles in 1919.

Under the Hague Convention, the United States passed its principal law about narcotics six years before the United Kingdom came to it. The Harrison Narcotics Act of 1914 was on its face a tax measure, but control, if not prohibition, was its aim, as the congressional hearings on the legislation made clear; the tax, which was a dollar a year, but which required physicians and pharmacists to register with the collectors of internal revenue and to keep detailed records, was merely a constitutional stratagem to preëmpt state regulation of the medical profession. The curious effect, though, was to entrust enforcement of America's national narcotics policy to the Treasury, where it stayed until 1968—and where it was joined for a while by enforcement of the national prohibition of alcoholic drink. The ban on heroin rested on the 1914 act but was not set out there: the Harrison Act said, ambiguously, that a doctor, after paying his yearly tax, could prescribe narcotics "in the legitimate practice of his profession" and "in good faith." Seizing upon this language, the Commissioner of Internal Revenue, between 1915 and the '20s, put out a series of ever-tightening regulations, and won a number of court decisions, which defined legitimate medical practice to squeeze

American doctors out of giving any kind of narcotic to any addict, whether to maintain his habit or to withdraw him from it gradually. The medical profession, particularly in Illinois and New York, protested almost in the terms of today's debates that addicts were diseased, not criminal, and that the ban was driving them to underworld supplies. Protests failed. In many cities, including Los Angeles and, notably, Shreveport, Louisiana, promising municipal clinics for morphine and heroin addicts were shut down by zealous Treasury Department action. The largest such clinic opened in New York City in April 1919, and had registered over seven thousand addicts by January 1920. That September, the Bureau of Internal Revenue began more strictly enforcing its policy against maintenance of addicts; the relapse rate among those taken off drugs was so discouraging that at the end of the year the clinic's administrators themselves recommended that the New York City clinic be closed. (The story of these American heroin clinics has recently been set out by David Musto in his book *The American Disease*, which is the first good history of the origins of American policies about addiction.) Total prohibition of heroin in the United States came almost as an afterthought, with the passage in 1924 of a one-sentence amendment to the Harrison Act, to forbid importation of opium for the purpose of making heroin.

In the years after that, the structure of treaties was repeatedly extended and elaborated, as the international traffic in narcotics increased and as new drugs presented addiction problems, so that, by 1953, nine different conventions, agreements, and protocols had been acceded to by various numbers of nations. In 1961, this tangle was codified and almost entirely replaced by the United Nations Single Convention on Narcotic Drugs. Similarly, and partly in conformance to the proliferating treaties, American law was patched and changed until it, too, was codified—and, in the process, extended—by two federal acts of 1970, the Comprehensive Drug Abuse Prevention and Control Act and the Controlled Substances Act. These replaced the Harrison Act and moved the Bureau of Narcotics from the Treasury to the Department of Justice; and, though they were illiberal laws—especially the Controlled Substances Act, drafted under the direction of an enforcement-minded Attorney General, John Mitchell—they also quietly rationalized the position of heroin. It is now no longer uniquely prohibited, but is classified as a Schedule I drug, along with LSD and others, with which clinical research is theoretically permitted, with the approval of the Food and Drug Administration and under the strictest controls. The change in heroin's technical legal status has simplified the assumptions of recent proposals to experiment with providing heroin legally to American addicts; but the psychological and political prohibition remains, so far, intact.

The British, once they had acceded to the Hague Convention, drafted control measures promptly. They began not far from where the Americans did. When Parliament came to debate the Dangerous Drugs Bill of 1920, a key issue of enforcement had already been settled in a brisk secret tussle between Sir Malcolm Delevingne, the top permanent official at the Home Office, and his opposite number at the Ministry of Health over which department should be responsible for control of the opiates and cocaine. (Cocaine, though not addictive and not an opium derivative, is treated just like one under international treaties, and by domestic law in both Great Britain and the United States.) The Home Office—the ungainly ministerial conglomerate that deals with, among many other things, police, prosecutions, and prisons—won the tussle; among its claims Delevingne asserted that "the matter is very largely a police matter." Thus, from the beginning to the present day, responsibility for watching over addiction has lodged primarily with the nearest British equivalent to the United States Department of Justice. The Dangerous Drugs Act, as passed, gave the government broad power to control the manufacture and use of narcotics; early regulations under the Act limited any doctor to supplying such drugs "so far only as is necessary for the practice of his profession." Thus a legal handle very much like the American one was available. It is clear that some people at the Home Office debated grasping that handle. Delevingne pressed the Ministry of Health repeatedly in the early '20s for "an authoritative statement"— one that he could take to court—from the leadership of the medical profession that the regular prescription of narcotics "without any attempt to treat the patient for the purpose of breaking off the habit, is not legitimate, and cannot be recognised as medical practice." Indeed, for a time in those years the Home Office was secretly circulating a list of suspected addicts and doctors to the police. Yet no prohibition evolved.

One reason was the British view of the American experience. It is certainly true that in the 1920s the British set their narcotics policy partly in response to what they saw happening in America—as they did again in the 1960s. Already in the Parliamentary debate in 1920, a backbencher, Captain Walter Elliot, charged that drug addiction was "an evil, spreading, I think, more from the United States than from any other country. It is also very interesting to remember that that is the great temperance country at the moment. . . . You have this effect, that they have gone in for prohibition and that they have developed the drug habit to an extent altogether unknown in this country." Elliot worked himself up to a denunciation of Americans as "the barbarians of the West" for their "extraordinary savage idea of stamping out all people who happen to disagree . . . with their social theories" against narcotics,

against alcohol—and in "their recent treatment of Socialists."
In January 1923, in *The British Journal of Inebriety,* Dr. Harry
Campbell reported what he had learned on a trip to the United
States; there, he said,

a drug habitué is regarded as a malefactor, even though the habit
has been acquired through the medicinal use of the drug. . . .
The Harrison Narcotic Law . . . placed severe restrictions on the
sale of narcotics and on the medical profession. In consequence of
this stringent law . . . the country is overrun by an army of
pedlars who extort exorbitant prices from their hapless victims. It
appears that not only has the Harrison Law failed to diminish the
number of drug-takers—some contend, indeed, that it has increased
their numbers—but, far from bettering the lot of the opium addict,
it has actually worsened it . . . impoverishing the poorer class of
addicts and reducing them to a condition of such abject misery as
to render them incapable of gaining an honest livelihood.

The warnings were heard.

"One has to see the treatment of the drug problem here in
the context of the style in which we carry on the public business," Dr. Edwards told me. "Not only through the government of the day but through the civil service. We have a strong
and highly esteemed civil service. It has the capacity and the
power to take the long view, beyond the term of one minister
or one government. I'm sure, for example, that the initial decision not to go the way of the Harrison Narcotics Act was a civil
service decision, which was then accepted by the politicians."

The other force in that decision was the medical profession.
The independence of British medicine is truly startling: its
jealousy of interference with its standards of practice is that of
a medieval guild, and the guild is effectively run by an oligarchy within the profession's top rank—the consultant physicians—who are individually often rich and collectively almost
unfettered. The question again is one of style in the public

business; the Rolls-Royces in Harley Street are very quiet cars. Americans have been reminded often enough that the postwar Labour government, led on the issue by Aneurin Bevan, socialized British medicine in 1946–47; British observers are likely to recall as well that Bevan could only create the National Health Service by making organizational and financial concessions that brought in—some would say, cast in concrete—the consultant oligarchy. The doctors have shaped British drug policy from its beginnings; in response to the intense, quiet pressure the Home Office was exerting in the early '20s, they quietly but adamantly maintained—as the opinion of the British medical profession—that "morphine and presumably heroin could not in all cases be totally withdrawn from a person addicted to these drugs. . . . Such an addict required a certain amount of the drug in order to keep him normal."

In 1924, civil servants and doctors got together. That September the government empanelled a blue-ribbon medical committee, under Sir Humphry Rolleston, baronet and president of the Royal College of Physicians, "to consider and advise as to the circumstances, if any, in which the supply of morphine and heroin . . . to persons suffering from addiction to those drugs may be regarded as medically advisable." In the next fifteen months, the Rolleston Committee met twenty-three times, taking oral evidence, in private, at seventeen of their meetings, from thirty-four witnesses, who included psychiatrists, apothecaries, a surgeon, general practitioners, professors of neurology, senior civil servants, the medical officers of Brixton and Pentonville prisons, two Scottish alienists, the Director of Public Prosecutions, and E. Farquhar Buzzard, Physician Extraordinary to H. M. the King. The committee wrote a thirty-six-page report, and in January of 1926 submitted it to the Minister of Health, who at the time was Neville Chamberlain. At the bottom of the introductory page was a note: "The cost of this Inquiry (including the printing of this Report) is estimated at £65. 5s. 6d." The expenditure bought forty-two years of policy.

The report of the Rolleston Committee is, for official prose, a minor marvel: clear, concise, and written in a sedate amble that eats up miles of law, administration, and medical opinion. Sir Humphry Rolleston was known for his energy and exactitude; he was in his early sixties, with a brilliant career ahead of him as well as behind, a man of high Victorian rectitude, patient, courteous, and aloof, with a towering reputation both as a pathologist and as a medical writer and editor. "His literary style, like his handwriting," says his biographer, "was as neat as an etching." His committee defined addiction with a precision that beats any of the other formal attempts I have read: an addict, the report said, is "a person who, not requiring the continued use of a drug for the relief of the symptoms of organic disease, has acquired, as a result of repeated administration, an overpowering desire for its continuance, and in whom withdrawal of the drug leads to definite symptoms of mental or physical distress or disorder." The report anticipated such unpleasant modern insights as that the hypodermic needle itself can acquire a compulsive attraction. It noted, and rejected with cool authority, what in the United States was by then not just medical opinion but the law, laid down in court decisions: that addicts "could always be cured by sudden withdrawal." It recognized that under any method of treatment "relapse, sooner or later, appears to be the rule."

The central issue of policy seems to have been put to the Rolleston Committee most starkly by Delevingne, of the Home Office: the object of medical treatment in cases of addiction must surely be "a steady diminution of the dose, with a view to its ultimate complete discontinuance." If so, wasn't the fact of continued administration in undiminished doses "evidence, *prima facie,* that the drugs were not being administered solely for the purposes of medical treatment"? No; the committee concluded that there were people "to whom the indefinitely prolonged administration of morphine or heroin may be necessary: those in whom a complete withdrawal of morphine or heroin produces serious symptoms which cannot be treated satisfactorily under the ordinary conditions of private practice, and those who are capable of leading a fairly normal and useful life so long as they take a certain quantity, usually small, of their drug of addiction, but not otherwise." Diagnosis of such need was up to the individual doctor—although he might not want to deal with such cases at all, and if he did so, he was warned, he would be wise to protect himself with a second medical opinion.

It is a fifty-year paradox that the American "enforcement model" chases after what is precisely a medical absolute—the seeming truth that cure should be the object, which means getting the addict off heroin—while the British have supposed that treatment of the addict, though exclusively the responsibility of doctors, should be predicated on a realistic view of what can and what cannot be enforced. For decades, such realism has been repeatedly excoriated by American officials responsible for control of narcotics; recently, for example, it was denounced as expediency, weakness, and surrender by, among others, the Director of the federal Bureau of Narcotics and Dangerous Drugs. But the report of the Rolleston Committee, when one reads it half a century later, has in fact the flavor of an almost Johnsonian conservatism, the sort of muscular pessimism that succeeds in being compassionate. The committee were the more able to be compassionate because—as the report said with an air of surprise—the evidence "is remarkably strong in support of the conclusion that, in this country, addiction to morphine or heroin is rare." No reliable estimates exist for the number of addicts in the early 1920s, either in England or in the United States. It is often said, by averaging everybody's guesses, that when it became illegal to prescribe narcotics to addicts in the United States, two hundred thousand people were affected—one in every five hundred. In Great Britain in 1925, while the Rolleston Committee was deliberating, thirty-five people, almost all of them Chinese, were prosecuted for the use of opium, and thirty-three people were prosecuted on charges of illegal use of morphine, heroin, or cocaine; the British population was then forty-five million.

.At times of great public anxiety about drugs and addiction—whether, for example, over opium smoking in the Far East in the nineteenth century or over heroin in the United States since the Second World War—the addict has often been seen through the wrong end of the telescope, separated, distanced, and diminished, as though in the grip of a force, the drug itself, that relentlessly destroys his body and degrades his moral independence. He is seen as an automaton, winding down. At such times, some addicts come to see themselves that way. The Rolleston Committee was a group of eminent doctors, hearing evidence for the most part from men of their own kind; they met at a time when public concern about addiction in England was not high. The addicts they envisioned, "to whom the indefinitely prolonged administration of morphine or heroin may be necessary," were not winding down, but stable—and stable more than in their daily dose, but socially stable, in their daily lives. The idea of the stable addict, defined if not named in that celebrated brief passage, has been the most durable contribution of the Rolleston Committee to the British approach to narcotics. Among their many other conclusions, two issues of administration concerned them. They heard strong suggestions that doctors be required to report new cases of addiction as they do the notifiable plagues like

smallpox; the committee concluded that the idea was an un-
called-for violation of "the confidential character of the relation of doctor and patient." So compulsory notification was not
established. The committee also considered whether there
ought to be a way for the Home Secretary, when a physician
was abusing the right to administer or prescribe narcotics, to
take away that right without more drastic action like taking
the man to court (which would mean "public odium," medically unqualified magistrates, and irrelevant sentences) or
taking him before the profession's governing body, the General Medical Council (whose only disciplinary recourse is to
disqualify the doctor from practice altogether). The committee
concluded that a permanent medical tribunal should be con-
stituted to judge such doctors and recommend restrictions on
their right to prescribe. But the idea lapsed and the tribunals
were not set up. Compulsory notification and medical tribunals
both reëmerged in the 1960s.

For many years, perhaps since the time of the Rolleston
Committee, one important fact about the rights of the addict
in Britain has been misunderstood. There has been an almost
indestructible belief that the addict can be in some way cen-
trally "registered" with the government, after which he is legally entitled to be maintained on his narcotic. That has never
been true—though the legend has caused many a newly hooked
English adolescent a jolting descent to earth, and regularly
confuses visitors. A recent example of the confusion appeared
in *Licit and Illicit Drugs: The Consumers Union Report,* a
sensible book that nonetheless says, of those English addicts
maintained on methadone at the present day, "Any one of those
patients can at any time decide to go back to heroin and have
a legal right to get it," which is the reverse of the fact. The
essential point is that choice of treatment was always the

doctor's; it still is. The English "registered addict" has never existed. The Rolleston Committee had rejected the idea that doctors should be required to report cases of addiction; but the Home Office civil servants were still left with the duty of preventing the illegal diversion of narcotics from medical use, and on them also devolved a treaty obligation to report once a year to the League of Nations (and now to the United Nations) on the extent of addiction in the United Kingdom. For this supervision a Drugs Branch was set up in the Home Office in 1934. The Drugs Branch relied on only one compulsory source of information: the records of all dealings in narcotics and other strong drugs, including prescriptions filled, which must be kept by retail pharmacists, and which are inspected by the police, stopping by unannounced at least twice a year. In London, four men from the Metropolitan Police check pharmacies full time. The pharmacists' records reveal the identity of any patient getting morphine or heroin regularly for long, and who his doctor is. The system was explained to me this way: "The average terminal cancer case only lasts about three months; to avoid picking up those, the police had instructions to report any case of regular supplies that had been going on for six months or so. The Drugs Branch then had an arrangement with the Ministry of Health, which has regional medical officers around the country, themselves doctors. One of these would go along to discuss the case with the prescribing doctor and report back—either that it was a case of genuine medical need or that it was now a case of addiction." Police and prison doctors, too, would let the Drugs Branch know whenever they came across an addict, and so did some general practitioners voluntarily.

New cases of addiction, suspected or confirmed, were listed in an index by the Drugs Branch. If other details about the

case could be discreetly gathered, they were added. The index
was begun in rudimentary form sometime early in the 1930s,
and is still maintained. It is a record unique in the world—
unique as a virtually total enumeration of a major nation's
experience with a major social problem during nearly half a
century, and unique, too, as an embodiment of governmental
self-restraint. The index has been the essential starting point
for several studies of addiction. It seems to have been kept
with scrupulous care for the addicts' privacy. It has itself been
the subject of learned articles. The index is maintained by five
government clerks in a cluttered room, and is nothing more
prepossessing than six stacks of card files, two of them newer
than the others, set on corners of a desk and a table. Each
addict's card shows at least his name, his aliases (if any) and
address (if known), his age and physical description, the drugs
he has been reported to take, when he started taking them, and
where and when he was first reported. Many reports turn out
to be repeat sightings. Each new addict is given a number.

In 1936, the first year the records included much detailed
analysis, just 616 addicts were known to the Home Office. Nine
out of ten were addicted to morphine. One in twenty was on
cocaine, one in twenty was addicted to heroin. Most of the
addicts had acquired their habits in the course of medical
treatment for something else. Almost half were women. "In
the nature of things, the addicts were usually in the fifty-plus
age group, they were scattered through the country in no
contact with one another, and in fact were no problem what-
soever," I was told. "Often, the addiction was a secret even
from the addict's husband or wife. An addict was known as
such only to his doctor, and to two civil servants and a clerk."
One hundred forty-seven of the addicts were themselves doctors. By 1953, the number of known addicts of any narcotic

had dropped to 290. Not since the First World War had there been any sign, either from addicts or through customs seizures, of systematic smuggling.

The extraordinary fact is that heroin addicts were so few up through the 1950s that one man at the Home Office was able to know most of the nontherapeutic cases personally, and to follow, individual by individual, incident by incident, the epidemic of heroin addiction that developed over the next fifteen years. The Drugs Branch takes up a corner of one floor of a large building in Westminster, where the corridor walls are lined with a linoleum-brown stone identified by a chiseled inscription as "British marble." From there, the branch deals with drug manufacture and trade; it has been headed by a succession of rising civil servants, but two key men have been there since shortly after the war. The first is Charles G. Jeffery, now Chief Inspector, a compact, graying man, who despite his title and a certain hardness of palm is not any kind of policeman; he inspects the pharmaceutical industry. The second, in the office next door, is Deputy Chief Inspector H. B. (Bing) Spear, who has a youthful unlined face, pale hair, and pale eyes; on his wall is a map of London stuck with pins showing the offices of doctors suspected of overprescribing drugs such as, most recently, amphetamines and barbiturates. From October 1964 to the summer of 1972, their immediate boss was Assistant Secretary Peter Beedle, a tall, jovial, subtle man, who perhaps epitomizes what is meant by the capacity and power of the British Civil Service to take the long view. Not all of Beedle's attention was given to narcotics; among other things he was concerned with cruelty to animals and the protection of wild birds. By civil-service rule, these men may not talk for quotation. Both Jeffery and Spear, however, have published professional reports on the rise in addiction; a score of sources in London confirm and amplify what they say.

Outside the Home Office, Spear is described as the man who for nearly two decades carried his own index in his head; even in the late '60s, when addiction was rising rapidly, he knew the addicts so well, I was told, that when a doctor with a new case telephoned him, Spear would listen to the physical description, ask a couple of questions, and identify the addict, giving his real name, his previous physician, the size of his usual prescription, the particular group of addicts he belonged to, where he lived, and, often, the girl he was living with and the person who had given him his first shot of heroin. What was even more remarkable, addicts looked on the Home Office as friend, confidant, and ally, turning to the Drugs Branch when they were in trouble with the police or at work, say, or for help when they were defeated by the social-welfare bureaucracy—or simply to find a pharmacist outside London where prescriptions could be cashed on a holiday. The strict American parallel would be a Washington addict's coming in off the street to ask one of the assistant directors of the Drug Enforcement Administration (latest reorganization of the Bureau of Narcotics) for help in dealing with the landlord. The increased number of addicts in England today and the development of the clinics make this kind of individual contact less easy and less necessary; yet it still happens, and English addicts, though they dislike and distrust the police nearly as much as addicts anywhere—for one thing, British laws against marijuana are toughly enforced—still regard the Home Office Drugs Branch highly.

About 1950, the only heroin addicts in England whose addiction was not an accidental result of medical treatment or who were not themselves doctors or nurses made up a circle in London of no more than twenty-five. Most of these had picked up the heroin habit abroad. Several were socially prominent. They were always able to find one or two private doctors willing to ignore the ethical questions of cure, of second opinions, of minimum doses. They did not proselytize. Their number had remained steady for years. In 1951 came the first sign of increase—the warning temblor that rattled the teacups and set the chandeliers to swaying. That year, on the night of April 24, a young man named Kevin Patrick Saunders, who came to be called Mark, and who had been employed in the pharmacy of a hospital just outside London, returned there, broke in, and stole 3,120 heroin tablets, 144 grams of morphine (over five ounces), and two ounces of cocaine—drugs worth, at cost, the equivalent of a hundred dollars. Before Scotland Yard arrested him, in September, Mark had peddled most of the heroin and cocaine around the jazz clubs that had grown up in Soho. Of those Mark ultimately infected, twenty were jazz musicians, and a number were black, including six Nigerians. From a notebook he carried, full of initials, the police were able to list fourteen people who had bought directly from Mark. Only two were already on the index. Over the next several years, the remaining twelve presented themselves to doctors as addicts, as did a lot of *their* contacts. Spear has traced the addiction of sixty-three people back along the transmission tree to Mark. Some were soon in jail; some left the country; a few quit; several disappeared; within a few years seventeen died, often nastily.

The stolen cocaine was bought by some of the same people who bought the heroin. Cocaine is a violent stimulant, with few and circumscribed medical uses. Taken simultaneously with heroin, as Mark's customers used it, cocaine is said to counter heroin's depressive effects and add zing to the euphoric high. The use of drugs in multiple and bizarre combinations, frequently switching from one to another, has marked the

English epidemic from the start, though "poly-drug abuse" (current medical jargon on both sides of the Atlantic) has figured in the States only in the last few years. But even with Mark's customers trickling through the index, in the early '50s the number of heroin users whose addiction was non-therapeutic—that is, not a by-product of medical treatment for something else—climbed no higher than thirty-seven known in any one year.

Then, on 18 February 1955, Major Gwilym Lloyd-George, son of a famous father and Home Secretary in Anthony Eden's Conservative government, replied to a Parliamentary question from a backbencher that the current licenses to manufacture heroin, when they expired at the end of the year, "will not be renewed. After that date licences will only be granted for the manufacture of such small quantities as may be required for purely scientific purposes and for the production of nalorphine." No further exports of the drug were to be authorized, either. But since the importation of heroin had been prohibited, as an elementary control measure, for many years, the announcement—though it mentioned directly neither addiction nor the drug's use in general medicine—signified that heroin was to be banned. The new policy would mean replacement of the medical view of heroin and its dangers by an unemphatic, British variant of the international enforcement approach. After ten months of increasingly rancorous controversy and a thrilling denouement, the policy proved to be no more than a digression; and yet the controversy fixed the nature of the British approach to heroin much more firmly than before.

To the government, the proposed ban did not seem at all momentous. Heroin, after all, was a drug of minor utility and evil reputation. The fact that a number of countries still permitted the manufacture of heroin and its use in medicine had been for years an irritant to the American Bureau of Narcotics;

the bureau's commissioner, Harry J. Anslinger, had held his post since it was established in 1930, and was a fundamentalist about stamping out the drug menace. Partly under American pressure, academic medical opinion internationally had been drifting toward the view that so many new substitutes were available that heroin was not irreplaceable. English medical opinion certainly appeared to be following this drift. In 1950, the British Pharmacopoeia Commission had concluded that the alternative drugs were suitable; after checking with the British Medical Association and the Medical Research Council, they dropped the entry for diamorphine in the 1953 edition of the *Pharmacopoeia*. Several times, the latest in July 1953, *The British Medical Journal* published articles about heroin clearly sympathetic with the idea that there was "an *a priori* case for its total abolition"; the 1953 article drew one solitary letter of protest. Meanwhile, Anslinger was pursuing his campaign through the United Nations and its various specialized agencies. In 1953, the sixth World Health Assembly—W.H.A. is the parliament of the World Health Organization—met in Geneva and among its business resolved, in response to the American lobbying, that "the abolition of legally produced diacetylmorphine . . . would facilitate the struggle against its illicit use." Next, in 1954, the United Nations Commission on Narcotic Drugs, on which Anslinger himself served as the American representative, voted that all countries should be asked to ban heroin. The British delegate abstained, but said he thought the United Kingdom would consider the request favorably. Then the question moved up the organization chart to the Economic and Social Council of the U.N., who resolved the same way.

In retrospect, the British government's acquiescence seems almost absent-minded: the formal machinery of policy making was switched on, but nobody was watching it. Iain Macleod,

Minister of Health at the time, first asked for the opinion of
the government's all-purpose Standing Medical Advisory Committee, which included Edward A. Gregg, chairman of the
Council of the British Medical Association, two other B.M.A.
leaders, the president of the General Medical Council, and
the presidents of the Royal College of Physicians and the other
collegiate organizations of specialists. The Standing Medical
Advisory Committee, when the question was put to them in
innocent-seeming but narrow form, whether heroin was in-
dispensable, replied unanimously that adequate substitutes
were available. So Macleod told Major Lloyd-George and the
rest of the cabinet that the Ministry of Health found no ob-
stacle to Britain's conforming to the U.N. resolutions. Thus,
out of a combination of international pressure and domestic
indifference, the decision was reached that after the end of
1955, the Home Office would issue no more licenses to manufacture. New legislation was unnecessary. When stocks ran
out, the use of heroin would cease.

The government was completely unprepared for the doctors'
reaction. An extraordinary battle now began. Senior physicians
denounced the ban—as astonishing and iniquitous, as sure to
produce "much hardship to a multitude of patients," as inter-
fering with treatment of addicts by gradual withdrawal from
heroin, as an unprecedented infringement of the liberty of
medicine. Letters in the medical weeklies derided the sup-
position that the heroin legitimately manufactured in Britain
had any effect on the world's illicit traffic. The list of pains for
which heroin was of peerless value grew longer. Many hospitals and general practitioners began stockpiling heroin for
years ahead. Macleod insisted in the Commons that he had
consulted medical opinion as he was required to do, but now
many doctors said that the Standing Medical Advisory Committee could not speak for the profession. On June 3, the

annual meeting of the British Medical Association passed
resolutions by large majorities calling for the manufacture of
heroin to continue. Dr. Gregg, chairman of the B.M.A.'s council, had concurred in the advice of the year before; now Gregg
said that of course he was not on the Advisory Committee as
a representative of his association. Gregg led a deputation
from the B.M.A. to see Lloyd-George and Macleod on July 11.
Privately, ministers and their civil servants were furious that
the leaders of the British Medical Association, as well as other
advisers, had switched sides. On October 17, Macleod wrote
the B.M.A. that the decision was irrevocable. Next, the twelve
London teaching hospitals announced that they unanimously
opposed the ban. The newspapers seized the issue and took
the doctors' side, from *The Times* to *The News of the World*.
On Monday, December 5, Macleod was put to the question in
the Commons; conceding only that "this decision is a desperately difficult one for a government to take," he asserted over
and over again that medical opinion had been consulted and
that the prohibition would stand. On Thursday, Lloyd-George,
less eloquent, was as adamant.

Five days later, on December 13, the prohibition was aban-
doned. That day the House of Lords was scheduled to debate a
motion, put down a while before by Earl Jowitt, that the current licenses to manufacture heroin should be extended beyond
December 31 until the conflict of medical opinion was resolved.
Under British constitutional arrangements, the House of Lords'
true importance is now as much in the judicial as in the legislative function. The Lords have been almost totally stripped
of effective legislative powers, so that what is said there about
bills to be passed is not often consequential; but among their
members are the Lord Chief Justice and the other justices—
the Lords of Appeal in Ordinary—who make up the nation's
highest court of appeals, while the Lord Chancellor, who pre-

sides over that highest court as well as over the House of Lords, is the most eminent legal officer of the government of the day. Retired Law Lords remain peers. (It is as though the present and retired members of the U.S. Supreme Court were automatically members of the Senate.) It was a legal argument that unexpectedly routed the government. Somebody, over the weekend, suggested to Lord Jowitt—himself a former Lord Chancellor—and the British Medical Association that they consider the exact language about licensing in the Dangerous Drugs Act. Who transmitted the suggestion has never been acknowledged; almost certainly the point originated with a civil servant inside the Home Office, who had noticed that the Act gave the Home Secretary licensing power as a means of controlling manufacture of the drug, but not, after all, in terms that could be stretched to include total prohibition. The day before the debate, Jowitt took up the question with the then Lord Chancellor, Viscount Kilmuir, who agreed. Lord Jowitt opened the debate. "There is very serious ground for doubting . . . whether the Home Secretary has any right to use this [the existing] Act as a vehicle for bringing about this ban," he told the peers. "If that is said to be a method controlling the manufacture to prevent its improper use, all I can ask is whether, if I were in charge of a horse, a dog or a child, and was told to control it, and I shot it through the heart, though it would lie still and give us no further trouble—should I really be controlling it?" (There were cheers.) The ban was beyond the powers of the Home Secretary; prohibition, Jowitt thought, would require a separate, new bill. He and the peers who followed then debated at full length the doctors' case against the ban. And if that was anticlimax, at times it was splendid: Lord Haden-Guest said that he had not been afraid on the battlefield, "There is too much girning and sob-stuff about death by cancer—I speak at the moment as a doctor," heroin was not the only way to relieve pain, and "Do you suppose we had heroin in the First World War when we were fighting in France?" Lord Teviot said that many peers were shocked greatly at Lord Haden-Guest's references to the First World War, and that "he should have seen some of the things that I saw in the dressing stations and the forward hospitals in the First World War, he would have wished to God we had had heroin to help us then!" Lord Amulree intervened to say that he had hardly ever used heroin in his hospital work, but had used it a lot on himself when he got one of his nasty coughs, which were intractable; he had tried substitutes, but "I like my little drop of heroin: it works very well for me"; he had taken it for twenty-five to thirty years but had not yet become an addict. (There was laughter.) Even while they spoke, the government were deciding that Jowitt's legal question was crucial, and that they would lose, embarrassingly, if the matter came to a vote. At the end of the debate, Viscount Woolton announced for the government that the licenses would, after all, be issued after December 31. Prohibition of heroin was never pressed again. The drug resumed its place in the *British Pharmacopoeia*. At a time when addiction was not a domestic problem, the government was reminded of what it should never have forgot about dealing with the medical profession, and the doctors rediscovered how they valued their professional liberties and what they really thought about the medical uses of heroin.

By 1959, the number of nontherapeutic heroin addicts on the index had crept up to forty-seven. Meanwhile, three decades and a war after the Rolleston Committee, another medical panel, with another physician-baronet, Sir Russell Brain, for chairman, was asked by the Macmillan government to look at habit-forming drugs anew. The Brain Committee labored under handicaps. Their instructions were very broad: to consider the possible abuse, not just of morphine and heroin (as the Rolleston Committee had done), but of newer, related strong analgesics, and beyond these they took on barbiturates, amphetamines, and even tranquilizers. Worry about misuse of these drugs was justified—for example, the amount of barbiturates prescribed in England had almost doubled between 1951 and 1959—but, as it turned out, the Brain Committee were both distracted and indecisive in their consideration of so many problems. Then, too, they worked with neither the urgency nor the exceptional common sense of the Rolleston Committee. Strangely, although senior officials of the Home Office were in close touch with the Brain Committee, nobody in the Drugs Branch inspectorate gave evidence. The committee felt no need to question the general complacency of the British medical profession about the control of heroin. As one man told me with remembered bitterness, "They said that everything in the garden was lovely." Indeed, the committee said, in particular, that there was "no cause to fear that any real increase" in addiction was occurring, that most addicts were stabilized, and that, although there had been two doctors in the previous twenty years who had prescribed carelessly or in excess, "in spite of widespread inquiry, no doctor is known to be following this practice at present." While they reminded their colleagues to get a second medical opinion before treating an addict, they strongly rejected any revival of the Rolleston Committee's plan for special medical tribunals that could discipline a doctor by withdrawing his right to prescribe. They saw no need for specialized centers for treatment of drug addiction. In this fashion, the Brain Committee missed the first detectable signs of trouble: it took two and a half years to produce a handwringing document that plumped for no change.

On the evening of 18 April 1961, with the report due out in a few weeks, Sir Russell Brain gave a preview of the committee's findings in a talk before a closed meeting of the Society for the Study of Addiction, in London. The timing could not have been more embarrassing. Though the numbers were not yet public, nor even known to many in Brain's audience of specialists, the fact was that in the previous year nontherapeutic heroin addiction had risen sharply: twenty-three new cases making a jump of 53 per cent in the total. Among these was the first case under the age of twenty. In 1961, heroin addiction was rising even faster, and by the end of the year there were nearly twice as many new cases as in 1960, bringing the total to 112 known addicts. They were almost all in London; the custom had begun for an addict, late in the evening, to take his prescription dated for the next day to one of the two pharmacies in London that stayed open around the clock, where he would wait with his mates for midnight. The junkie coven at Boots the Chemists in Piccadilly Circus became a grisly tourist attraction and was parodied in films. In Brain's audience at the Society for the Study of Addiction was a pharmacist, Irving Benjamin, who worked at the other all-night shop—John Bell & Croyden, Wigmore Street. Benjamin had kept his own card file with data on each addict who came in with a prescription. After Sir Russell's anodyne assurances that there was only a small and apparently diminishing number of addicts, "scattered about the country," and a negligible illicit traffic in their drugs, Benjamin stood up. As one who was there described it, "Benny caused a little bit of a hoo-ha."

"Sir Russell's optimism amazes me," Benjamin began. "A short while ago, I came across an addict who was completely unknown to the Home Office. He presented his prescription to a shop for something like thirty grains of cocaine [1,800 milligrams] and forty to fifty grains of heroin. That was repeated on several different occasions, in several quantities. This was prescribed by a doctor who I know for a fact was making every

HOW THE PROBLEM LOOKED IN 1960–61

	1936	1940	1945	1950	1955	1956	1957	1958	1959	1960	1961
All addicts of all narcotics [1]	616	505	367	306	335	333	359	442	454	437	470
Doctors, allied professions	147	90	80	95	86	99	88	74	68	63	61
All heroin addicts				[a]	54	53	66	62	68	94	132
Therapeutic (originating in treatment for something else)					18	17	21	19	21	22	20
Nontherapeutic					**36**	**36**	**45**	**43**	**47**	**72**	**112**
Heroin addicts aged under 20					none known					1	2
New heroin addicts that year (nontherapeutic)				1	9	9	5	8	9	23	54

[1] The Home Office grand total includes people addicted to morphine, and—after the Second World War—pethidine, dextromoramide, and other morphine-related drugs or synthetics as these were introduced into medical practice. Until 1945, cases were kept on the index for ten years after the last information received, except deaths; beginning in 1958, index totals include only those people known to have been taking drugs in the year in question.

[a] Exact numbers of addicts of the various narcotics were not broken down before 1955, but the proportion of addicts using heroin varied from 5 per cent in 1935 to 19 per cent in 1952.

effort to treat these people. . . . That patient had obviously been obtaining supplies illicitly on such a scale as to get used to those quantities. . . . As to the suggestion that there seems to be no large center of addiction, I personally can record forty or fifty cocaine, heroin, and morphine addicts in the London area alone."

The problem that alarmed Benjamin was indeed becoming a medical scandal; over the next eight years, as the scandal ran its course, the lives of a thousand patients were wrecked, many died, and several doctors were ruined. "Anybody who goes to an illegal source for his drug is a fool," another man called out from the floor of the meeting where Benjamin spoke. "There cannot be a very big black market in Britain, simply and solely because the laws are as they are, and not as they are in America." But that was the last protest of complacency, for, in fact, one consultant at a drug clinic recently recalled, "It was perfectly possible then to maintain a habit at a modest financial outlay without having to go to the doctor oneself." New addicts were buying drugs from other addicts who were getting them, sometimes in unbelievable quantities, on prescriptions from general practitioners: the prescription system, which in the past had always kept the heroin supply in balance with the demand, so that a black market had nothing to feed on, had now become the only source of heroin for a black market so virulent that over one stretch the number of heroin addicts on the Home Office index was doubling every sixteen months. And for the first time there was real fear that the index was missing many addicts.

The reasons for the English heroin epidemic are still bitterly argued, for they are by no means altogether clear. Blame has been shared out among the doctors who were prescribing to addicts; the rest of the medical profession, who turned their backs on the incipient problem; the addicts themselves, who were a type that doctors had not had to deal with before; the other drugs adolescents were taking, or that their *parents* were taking; television and the press, for publicizing those drugs; and the more fundamental revolution in youth's customs, beliefs, roles in the social order, and powers of influencing each other which was going on (apparently in all industrialized countries) in the 1960s. Any halfway satisfactory accounting of the English epidemic promises help in interpreting the social mechanisms in other drug crazes, like the amphetamine plague that swept Japan in the '50s or the manic use of stimulants that still afflicts some groups of young Swedes; and, obviously, the English heroin epidemic rightly understood should illuminate, if only by contrast, the American heroin problem. More than that, only by disentangling the causes of the English epidemic can one come to see clearly how it was at last brought under control.

The English argument begins—though it doesn't end—with the doctors in the '60s who were writing prescriptions for addicts. They were the first and easiest to be attacked, because they were the most visible. Some of them were obviously culpable. Even now, the names of the "prescribing doctors" are mentioned reluctantly by officials or by colleagues who observed what was happening. Ten or twelve doctors were implicated at one time or another. Their motives varied. Most were in private practice rather than in the National Health Service. A few were venal, selling the prescriptions for cash to anyone glib enough who came to their offices. One was a compulsive gambler, who after a bad day with his turf accountant was known to make house calls on addicts. Another is now in Broadmoor, the English hospital-prison for the criminally

insane. Some were warped by the special relationship with patients which heroin makes possible: there were incidents,
reported by psychiatrists who inherited the patients, of addicts
forced to crawl across the room on their bellies to get their
prescriptions. And a few of the prescribing doctors were dedi-
cated physicians attempting to treat patients that most doctors
refused to touch. The Drugs Branch often tried to warn doctors
off, but whenever one doctor dropped out, the addicts swarmed
to another. Over the years, the Home Office and the most active
or conscientious of the prescribing doctors developed a col-
laboration: the doctors helped keep up the index, and the
inspectors stayed in touch with the network of addicts as the
infection spread.

The insidious role that doctors' motives can play in the
treatment of drug addicts is a theme that runs through the
British experience to the present day. The problem is now
becoming evident in the United States, too, with the growth
of methadone-maintenance programs; in the past couple of
years several privately run treatment centers, in New York,
Chicago, and elsewhere, have had to be shut down because the
physicians in charge began handing out methadone in large
amounts, indiscriminately. What can be involved when a doctor prescribes narcotics was suggested in the course of a conversation I had with Martin Mitcheson, a bearded, engagingly
quizzical psychiatrist, with a law degree as well, who runs the
drug-dependence clinic at University College Hospital. Dr.
Mitcheson was on the telephone as I came in, evidently talking
with a court official about one of his patients. "Not much possible for a year or two yet," he was saying, with clipped concern. "I'll just have to grip the arms of my chair and hope she
turns up . . . using the prescription as some kind of control.
. . . I'm sure she will go back to prison, but I think that this

is a bad case to recall her on." After he hung up, we began
by talking about the incidents of the early '60s. " 'The Psychopathology of the Prescribing Doctor'—that's a paper that will
never be written," Mitcheson said. "And one reason it won't
be written is that I am on the same continuum as those doctors
were—though, one hopes, in a less extreme position. But I am
in a position with a great deal of power. For instance, that
phone call just now was about one of my addicts, a girl I am
keeping out of prison on this occasion. But after that she is not
going to get her prescription unless she goes through certain
hoops for me. The control that prescribing offers, on top of the
relationship that develops with a patient anyway—as a psychiatrist one has a duty to be aware of this. And maybe one can
use it a bit. But some of the prescribing doctors, I think, were
totally out of control of their own psychopathologies—completely at their mercy—and did the most dreadful amount of
harm."

One of the first and most notorious of the prescribing doctors
was Lady Isabella Frankau. She had a private practice in Wim-
pole Street, is said to have been moderately successful in treating alcoholism, and certainly did not need to work with addicts
for any reason like the money in it. Among her earliest drug
patients were a number of the jazz musicians—including several of the Nigerians—who had become addicted in the '50s;
Lady Frankau was a principal instrument in pumping that
group up into the fulminating heroin outbreak of the '60s. She
dominated the personal lives of some of her patients. Such
domination is essentially ambiguous. "Addicts are motivated,
highly manipulative, lying psychopaths," one doctor told me.
"Lady Frankau was hoodwinked." In 1960 she and a colleague
published a paper in *The Lancet* on the treatment of drug
addiction, in which they reported cases maintained on heroin
and cocaine during an extended preliminary period of psycho-

therapy before withdrawal was attempted. The paper spoke
with ominous naïveté about prescribing to addicts:

A minor difficulty during this period was their inability to say
simply that they had overstepped the usual amount. Instead they
either augmented their supplies from the black market, or produced plausible stories of accidents or losses. Eventually they real-
ised that it was better to state bluntly that too much had been
used. Extra supplies were prescribed to prevent them returning to
the black market, which would involve them in financial difficulties,
and (which is even more important) would mean a return to the
degradation and humiliation of contacting the pedlars. . . . During this phase of treatment the patients acquired enough insight
into their condition to be able to cooperate.

"Extra supplies" brought some of Lady Frankau's patients up
to 1,800 or 2,400 milligrams of heroin a day, and while some
were really injecting nearly that much a day—a three- or even
six-month supply for an American addict—most were pushing
out the surplus. In 1962, Lady Frankau alone prescribed six
kilograms of heroin: more than thirteen pounds.

John Hewetson and Robert Ollendorff, in contrast, were in
general practice together, not privately but under the National
Health Service. They had had three or four addicts among their
patients for several years, so they later wrote in *The British
Journal of Addiction,* and from them learned "that there were
a vast number of addicts who were able to get their prescriptions privately, but who were frightened to bring their addiction problem to their [N.H.S.] general practitioner, and who
therefore bought their drugs on the Black Market." Believing
that their colleagues were making it impossible for addicts to
get care under the National Health Service, to which they were
entitled like any other patient, Hewetson and Ollendorff decided to take on any genuine addict who came to them. Within
six months they had nearly a hundred. Their account makes

vivid the exasperating irritations that doctors met, and the risks they ran, in trying to treat addicts in such numbers as part of a general practice: the addicts' incessant demands, the ever-repeated mindless search for the next fix, the tantrums in crowded waiting rooms, the high rate of sickness, the endless night and weekend emergencies. "Clearly the work involved is so great that normally the general practitioner in a busy practice would be unable to cope with it at all," they wrote. Even for doctors with the soundest motives, a hundred heroin addicts create pressures that after a while distort judgment.

By the end of 1964, the index carried 329 nontherapeutic addicts, 160 of whom had been added just that year; 40 were under the age of twenty, including one child of fourteen. In 1965, the total jumped to 509; in 1966, to 885, more than 300 of them under twenty. Not only the rate of increase but the actual numbers began to look scary. The prescribing doctors were blamed by the press and in official inquiries. But clearly that blame was too indiscriminate. "None of those doctors were getting any help," I was told by one official who had known them. "They weren't even getting the backing of hospitals. I mean, if you want to level a criticism it must be at all the rest of the profession, who were not prepared to take their share of the load." This observation marks about the furthest point that any public analysis of the problem had reached by the mid-'60s. The change to addiction clinics was designed expressly and narrowly to put prescribing general practitioners out of the heroin business, to shift the responsibility for maintaining addicts to a more controllable part of the medical profession, consultant psychiatrists, and to give those who were now to be dealing with addicts some formal institutional supports—a hospital setting, regular touch with professional colleagues.

Only one English doctor who was treating addicts in general practice during the mid-'60s is still in the field. He is Peter

HOW THE PROBLEM LOOKED AS THE CLINICS WERE BEING SET UP

	1958	1959	1960	1961	1962	1963	1964	1965	1966	1967
All addicts of all narcotics	442	454	437	470	532	635	753	927	1,349	1,729
All heroin addicts	62	68	94	132	175	237	342	521	899	1,299
Therapeutic	19	21	22	20	18	15	13	12	13	9
Nontherapeutic	**43**	**47**	**72**	**112**	**157**	**222**	**329**	**509**	**885**	**1,290**
Heroin addicts aged under 20	none	1	2	3	3	17	40	134	317	381
New heroin addicts that year (nontherapeutic)	8	9	23	54	72	90	160	258	518	745

The Home Office grand total, across the top line, includes people addicted to morphine, pethidine, dextromoramide, and other morphine-related drugs or synthetics; most of these are addictions originating in medical treatment for something else.

Chapple, a psychiatrist, whose careworn and comfortable manner belies the fact that he has long been bitterly critical of English drug policies. Dr. Chapple has turned against heroin for addicts; he now runs two programs, one using methadone and the other requiring total abstinence, in the part of London that has been known since Restoration days, with reason, as World's End. Looking back, in conversation, Chapple said, "There were several very disturbed doctors dealing with the addicts. Yet the campaign against the doctors was unfair, for there were also one or two very good men, quite skillful at handling addicts, among the general practitioners. Everybody was naïve, though; we all did all sorts of silly things. But was it really the prescribing doctors who created the problem? Or was it in fact that we were getting a new type of addict, who had come from a very different place?" His questions open up the next layer of the problem: in the interaction between prescribing doctors and their addict patients in the '60s, the big change was not in the doctors—addicts had always found doctors—but in the addicts.

On the simplest descriptive level, accounts of the epidemiology of heroin in England have often begun by noting the early ubiquity of other, supposedly milder drugs among the youth. Spear, of the Home Office, wrote that the first heroin outbreak —Mark's, back in 1951—came after a summer when vigorous police action had created a temporary scarcity of cannabis (marijuana or its resin). In 1960, there was a widespread fashion among adolescents, particularly working-class, particularly in London, for amphetamines and barbiturates; most typically, these were taken in combination, in the pills marketed by Smith, Kline & French as Drinamyl but called by users and the press "purple hearts," because they were blue and triangular. Teen-agers would come to central London for a weekend and eat pills to stay up for sixty hours dancing. "Drinamyl was our particular thing, actually," Chapple recalled. "The pills were black-marketed for a shilling each. They had been a standard treatment for depression. For many years. By established psychiatrists. So this was a 'reasonable' drug to give people, and it was given very widely. And kids experimented with them. They were used by mods and rockers. They were popularized by the press. And if you're an adolescent, and you can take a pill and don't have to put up with your adolescent depression . . ." He shook his head.

Looked into, though, the use of other drugs by English adolescents, with one vicious exception in 1967 and 1968, turns out to have nothing demonstrably to do with their use of heroin. The idea that one drug leads to another—the escalation theory—has great plausibility. It is popular in the United States among those, from the President on down, who oppose legalizing marijuana. It is not believed by many American doctors or social workers with day-to-day experience, nor is it supported by what research has been possible. In England, escalation is sometimes preached in the House of Lords from the more tenebrific Tory back benches. Professionals reject it—Home Office specialists, clinic psychiatrists, and research sociologists alike. They cite, for example, the fact that immigrants from the West Indies, Pakistan, and India, who were among the first people in England to use marijuana, have always been surprisingly rare among heroin addicts. Then, too, those drug-using adolescent groups in London were so little overlapping, according to Kenneth Leech, who was curate of the parish of St. Anne, Soho, and who conceived it his mission to minister to the drifting youth, dropouts, pill-takers, and addicts, that "until about 1966 it was possible to divide Soho, drugwise, into the 'junkie' scene at the Piccadilly end and the 'pill-head' scene north of Shaftesbury Avenue. There was little contact between the two groups." Yet the ghost of the escalation theory lingers in the belief that those years saw a change of attitude among young people—widespread, amorphous, climatic—which fostered experimentation with mood-changing substances; in Chapple's phrase for the phenomenon, "chemical problem-solving by the young."

Young English heroin addicts have been unlike their pill-taking or marijuana-smoking cousins; they have also been unlike their American brothers. "Our explosion went the other way from yours," I was told by one authority. "Yours started among the deprived ethnic minorities, in the main, but now is spreading up and out into the white middle-class suburbs, or so one gathers. When we first began to come out of that exclusively jazz-musical circle, in 1960, we started getting the middle-class would-be hippies—we called them pseudo beatniks then—and only later went down to the working class."

English investigators are persuaded that their middle-class addicts, at least, have been more profoundly disorganized, disturbed, and ineffectual than is generally true in the United States. They have also tended to be younger. Working-class addicts began to turn up in significant numbers only in 1964 and after. Dr. Margaret Tripp, a psychiatrist who worked for three years at the end of the '60s with several hundred working-class addicts at a clinic in East London, told me, "Compared to the West End dropout crowd, mine were not so different from the population from which they came. They were much nearer to the stereotype of the kid that gets nothing from the school in the working-class area. Truancy, then petty stealing, a joy ride in a car, typically at least one appearance before the magistrate. Then drugs, any or all that were available, including heroin once it came on the street."

English patterns of heroin addiction differ from American not only in relation to social class but, even more, in relation to race. Several English cities have slums with alien communities—Pakistanis, Indians, and Bengalis; black West Indians; a few Africans—large enough to be cohesive and sometimes inflammatory presences. Yet nonwhite addicts remain disproportionately rare. English narcotics users, virtually without exception after the jazz musicians, have been white. The fact stands in instructive contrast, of course, to the United States, where some people have seriously argued that blacks are genetically predisposed to addiction, and where, for example, recent figures in New York City estimate that blacks, though they are only twenty per cent of the city's population overall, account for forty to forty-five per cent of the addicts.

The connection between addiction and crime in England is more problematic. Certainly crime rates there are low compared to the United States. In particular, the quick and brutal banditry that terrorizes New York or Washington, so easily blamed on junkie desperation, is almost unknown in London—though the American newcomer needs months to extinguish his fear of certain configurations of strangers along a sidewalk, which in the States he would read as a signal to turn away but which in Soho or Notting Hill mean no danger and can be walked straight through. It is also true—and is the most seductive argument for trying heroin maintenance in the United States—that an English addict need not steal to support his addiction. The British police concede this, though they are by no means inclined to be tolerant of drugs or drug users. The man at Scotland Yard in charge of drug crime until mid-1973 (as well as counterfeiting and the murder and bomb squads) was Commander Robert Huntley, up from the ranks, decorated for bravery by the Queen. Huntley, tending the stub of a cigar and talking of cannabis, could be taken for one of his opposite numbers at the Bureau of Narcotics and Dangerous Drugs. "Our problem is not really heroin," he said in his London office early in 1973. "Drug addicts have an inherent

proneness to commit crime," he insisted, "but there is really
no evidence in this country that drug addiction as such causes
its victims to resort to crime to obtain money. This is largely
due to our maintenance program." Nonetheless, as every English study to touch on the point has demonstrated, there is an
unquestionable link between addiction and delinquency. The
point seems to be, though, that the delinquency begins months
or often years before the addiction, and that addict crime in
England is petty and passive. "The crime was pretty small
stuff, usually," Dr. Tripp said of her experience among working-class addicts. "These weren't the most aggressive ones; the
ones that got onto heroin couldn't live up to the image of a
man in the East End." Conversations with English addicts
quickly disclose that those who hustle rather than work are
more likely to be beggars than thieves. Ian Pierce James,
formerly the medical officer at Brixton Prison, in South London,
wrote in 1970 that English addicts were "young, highly unstable, sociopathic, multiple-drug users . . . characterized by
a high degree of delinquency, which was not an outcome of
their addiction but usually preceded it." Yet, he wrote, "the
addicts in our study were, on the whole, markedly inefficient
criminals." In a later conversation, Dr. Pierce James noted,
"These drug-blocked kids couldn't steal enough to support a
habit on a black market like New York."

On 23 December 1959, an addict from Canada, where heroin
is illegal, arrived in England. He was unable to find a doctor
right away, developed severe withdrawal symptoms, and spent
the Christmas holidays in a London hospital. The next August
two more Canadian addicts came to England; by the end of the
next decade ninety-one addicts had immigrated from Canada.
Spear, of the Drugs Branch, wrote in 1971, in *The British
Journal of Addiction,* that a number of the Canadians, "show-

ing how firmly established in North American minds was the concept of the 'British system,' voluntarily 'reported' at the Home Office within hours of landing at London airport." Many of the Canadian addicts first learned from Lady Frankau that heroin was legal and available in England; she made a lecture tour across Canada in 1963, describing her method of treating addicts. These Canadians have sometimes been blamed for starting the English heroin epidemic, though most of them arrived later than that, and for building up the black market, though a number of them soon left, saying that they missed the excitement of the illegal pursuit of narcotics and that pure English heroin did not deliver the kick of the adulterated stuff they were used to. Those who stayed in England are unique, because they have lived as addicts under both approaches to heroin. In 1969, Jim Zacune, an American sociologist then at the Addiction Research Unit in London, began to try to trace the Canadian addicts. He found that ten had died in England, ten more had been deported, thirty-five appeared to have left voluntarily, and some had vanished; but he did reach twenty-five of those still in England. The twenty-five were in some obvious ways a very biased sample, since all of them had shown that they could get along—minimally, at any rate—in England. They were, as well, very different from the native English addicts at the treatment clinics: they averaged more than fifteen years older, had been addicted to heroin nearly four times as long, and were taking three and a half times as much, their daily doses averaging 597 milligrams, or just under ten grains. Despite all that, the contrast is extraordinary between the twenty-five Canadians' lives as addicts in Canada and in England. Thus, though they were not important as a cause of the English heroin problem, their histories suggest some interesting things about the advantages of living where addiction is not criminal. Twenty of the

Canadians were men, of whom only one claimed to have worked steadily in Canada while he was addicted; of the five women, two had worked briefly as secretaries, one had been a telephone operator, one a student, and one a housewife. But in England thirteen of the twenty-five were employed full time, and had held their present jobs between six months and seven years. ("And that *last* one," Zacune said later, "was on nine grains of heroin a day throughout the seven years, and in all the time had hardly missed two days from his job washing taxis in Putney.") In Canada, the twenty-five addicts had been convicted a total of 182 times—an average of more than seven times each—including eighty-eight times for some form of theft. In Canada, they had spent a total of 141 years and 2 months in prison—an average of nearly seven years each—even though the group included two who had served no time at all. Of the total number of years that the twenty-five had lived in Canada after becoming addicted, almost one year out of four had been spent in prison. In England, though six of them had done time there, too, the combined total was two years and five months—which was less than one year out of fifty of the total time they had lived, still addicted, since immigrating.

As the number of English addicts grew, thoughtful physicians began to see that they represented a much more complex and tragic problem—on purely medical grounds—than had been recognized. The new addicts were sick and dying people. A consultant psychiatrist who realized this about his own patients was Thomas Bewley, an Irishman, short, with a crew cut, staccato of speech and manner, who now directs the drug-dependence clinics at Lambeth Hospital, south of the Thames, and Tooting Bec Hospital, even farther south near Brixton Prison. In 1961, Bewley had opened an inpatient unit for alcoholics at Tooting Bec, and by 1964 had treated a score of heroin addicts there, which in those days was a lot of experience. Bewley combed the Home Office index and reported in *The British Medical Journal* that in the mid-'60s "the mortality rate among 'non-therapeutic' addicts was twenty-eight times the expected rate and chiefly due to sepsis [infections from unsterile injection], overdose, and suicide," while "for every thirty-seven addicts known to the Home Office each year there is one death." The average age of addicts' death was dropping into the low twenties. Sickness and hospitalization rates were similarly bad.

The planets were wheeling again into the conjunction of 1924; the consultant physicians were lining up with the civil servants. The latter, and in particular the Drugs Branch inspectorate, had been pressing for changes at least since the Brain Committee published its report; but, as one of them said recently, "It took us until 1964 to persuade our masters that the situation really did need looking at." What the changes should be, though, was not self-evident to those who had to propose policies. The three-point package that eventually emerged—addiction-treatment clinics, with no doctor outside the clinics allowed to prescribe heroin or cocaine to addicts, and with all doctors required to notify the Home Office of new cases—appears so neat that it gives the British Civil Service credit in this instance for the wrong sort of skill. What creates the illusion of a deliberate piece of social engineering was in reality a resolution of conflicting forces and requirements—an adroit political achievement. Perhaps the most important requirement was not to react too strongly. In England in 1964, one observer told me a decade later, "The machinery for dealing with addiction was thirty or forty years old. Despite the rise in addiction, very few doctors even knew the drugs or had ever seen an addict; the forensic scientists were much more concerned with alcohol; there were no police drug squads outside London, and even the drug squad at the Metropolitan Police was only a few men. And then there was this devoted band in the Home Office, specialized, somewhat self-taught, rather isolated, and because they dwelt in drugs night and day, they tended to have a narrow perspective. In such a context of fresh beginnings, I suspect it was very much easier than it might have been for any administrator, not exactly to take his time, or delay unduly, but to keep on testing the temperature and applying his mind to the question of *systems*. There were no systems." The United States in 1964, meanwhile, was discovering its own epidemic; from England what was happening in America looked explosive and, as usual, ominous. "It is impossible to exaggerate the dominance of the American drug scene in our thinking then—its dominance and its alleged *closeness*: a new drug would be reported in San Francisco one day and within a week there'd be overdoses of that same drug rumored in London. But this was largely anecdotal. Unsupported gossip. And yet one had the pressure of the American experience for years."

The Drugs Branch of the Home Office then numbered just five inspectors, and dropped to four in April 1965. They proposed, however, to buy computers and require drug manufacturers and suppliers to report their transactions, so that every movement of every narcotic could be monitored. They asked, of course, for more men, urged close ties with the police, the military, and the customs, and talked of special task forces. "From that side," I was told, "there was, for quite a time, the strong wish to build something like the American Bureau of Narcotics." The vision was resisted at levels higher up. In 1968, two more inspectors were at last added, for a total of six. (Today there are eleven.) Pressure for dramatic action came from outside, too, though it was loosely organized.

Some doctors and educators called for prevention, including
even compulsory urine tests for school children. They wanted
massive new powers for the police. "They wanted to close
Soho!"

Sanity's best friend was doubtless the cultivated caution of
English civil servants. There was no great pressure, either,
from ministers and politicians. A few made alarmed speeches.
"But the political tide was slackening. There were surprisingly
many who could see the real lesson of the American example,
that perhaps one had to accept that, after all, one could not
win this one. Certainly not in a year or two; not in the life of
a Parliament. So drugs never became a front-rank social problem in ministerial eyes. The key speeches were not uncon-
cerned, but they were cool. Furthermore, I don't think public
attention ever got agitated, seriously, at that period. There
was then, and there is now, very much less concern about
drugs than about cruelty to children or to animals; the Home
Office got ten letters about animals for every one about drugs
—and not that great a number in any case. So it was possible
to build an inhabitable structure of relative values and
urgencies. We were always aware, I think, of the danger that
if you create a response to a problem, then you have the
problem. And what in fact happened is that our response never
became very muscular."

In July 1964, the Brain Committee, having got things wrong
the first time, was reconvened by the government. Its chairman had meanwhile been raised to the peerage. Lord Brain
agreed to look again, but only under a narrow set of instructions: the target was to be the prescribing doctors. The second
Brain Committee took thirteen months. They pondered five
years' new statistics, and listened to experts—some whom they
had previously ignored, some jumped up in those five years.
Jeffery and Spear of the Drugs Branch argued before the Brain

Committee for the least and simplest adjustment to the rules for prescribing heroin. They pointed out that the best of the doctors dealing with addicts had irreplaceable experience; in order to protect the best and neutralize the worst, they recommended that no general practitioner should be allowed to treat more than a certain small number of addicts, and that second medical opinions should be made compulsory in cases of addiction, so that every new patient would be seen by a consultant psychiatrist as well as his general practitioner, and his dose of heroin be set by agreement between the two physicians. Some observers thought they detected in the Drugs Branch's conservatism the urge of an intelligence-gathering organization to maintain its familiar network of contacts and sources, as well as "a pretty strong loyalty to the rascals"; but certainly very few people in British medicine had the experience from which to argue that a different system would work. One of the few was Dr. Bewley, who, besides his surveys of mortality and morbidity among addicts on the index, was still regularly treating addicts as inpatients. In testimony to the committee, later published as a paper in *The Lancet,* Bewley outlined the essential features of the change to drug clinics that was becoming the consensus of the medical profession.

The consensus was reached, though, more outside the Brain Committee's meetings than in; and it was hastened by the unspoken recognition that the medical profession had badly failed to discipline itself. For the doctors to move at all against a colleague required that the General Medical Council find the man guilty of "infamous professional conduct" and strike him from the Medical Register, thus disqualifying him from practice. The machinery was too cumbersome, the penalty too absolute. The idea of notification—compulsory reporting of new cases of addiction—had been rejected by the Rolleston Committee and had not even been mentioned in the first

Brain Report; as much as ever, it would be a breach of the confidential relationship between doctor and patient, and there were not many models for it, even in public-health medicine. But—as Griffith Edwards, at the Addiction Research Unit, suggested to me—in several intangible ways the relation between the doctor and the addict patient had shifted since Rolleston. "Notification is a sign of the prejudiced autonomy of the medical profession," Edwards said. "Doctors are now almost all employees of the state. And between the '20s and the '60s there was a marked change in the social distance between doctor and addict; where the addict then was one's private patient—an infirm gentlewoman one had been treating for years, or old Baron von Something, or perhaps one's own wife—in the '60s the addicts could be seen as young miscreants, very different in age, class, education and so on." At the same time, another observer said, compulsory notification, together with the ban on prescribing heroin to addicts outside the clinics, offered a way to deflate the rhetoric of professional self-discipline down to a simple question of rules. The English style in conducting the public business can be almost invisible: "When one is negotiating with groups like the British doctors," I was told, "there are things that one doesn't say though they are things that one means."

The Brain Committee had aged badly. Their second report, when it came, sometimes drifted into querulous irrelevance: "Witnesses have told us that there are numerous clubs, many in the West End of London, enjoying a vogue among young people who can find in them such diversions as modern music or all-night dancing. In such places it is known that some young people have indulged in stimulant drugs of the amphetamine type." As best they could, the committee cleared the medical profession in general of blame; they calmed the fears fluttering the correspondence pages of *The Lancet* and *The*

British Medical Journal that the doctors' right to prescribe
without restriction for ordinary patients might be in danger.
They stated, in its simplest form, the conflict that has always
shaped British drug policy, between the individual addict as
a medical patient and the overall protection of the community.
"If there is insufficient control it may lead to the spread of
addiction—as is happening at present," they wrote. "If, on the
other hand, the restrictions are so severe as to prevent or
seriously discourage the addict from obtaining any supplies
from legitimate sources it may lead to the development of an
organized illicit traffic." Then the committee briskly ratified the
steps that the medical profession had already agreed were
necessary. These steps, turned into law, became the "clinic
system." The committee also thought the new treatment centers should have the power to detain addicts compulsorily,
though only for short periods. The idea was a dithery com-
promise between what the committee understood to be American experience that addicts, to be cured, must be institution-
alized for long stretches, and native British reluctance to
interfere with the addict's personal liberty. Reluctance won.
Such a provision was never enacted.

Who was to run the treatment centers? Where? How? The
Brain Committee had not said. Nobody really wanted the job;
the consultant psychiatrists proved extremely reluctant to take
it on. Parliament took two years to legislate the compulsory
notification of new cases and the restriction on prescribing to
addicts outside the treatment centers. The centers themselves
could have been organized immediately, under the National
Health Service; their establishment was repeatedly announced, repeatedly delayed, and at the last huddled
through. By then it was the end of 1967, and the number of
nontherapeutic heroin addicts known to the Home Office had
risen to 1,290. Lady Frankau died that year, but two new

and strangely motivated private doctors—Christopher Michael Swan and John Petro—had begun writing large scripts for heroin and cocaine. Dr. Swan, who was described to me as a big, good-looking man with an unformed face, had his surgery, with no partner, in the iron-hard hub of the working-class East End. He became increasingly obsessed by his addict patients, and was alternately their champion and their victim; one day his office erupted in violence; Swan went to prison and then went mad. Dr. Petro had no surgery at all, but was meeting addicts and writing prescriptions in the pubs and tearooms that are on the platforms of several stations of the London Underground. He charged three pounds each prescription. The *Daily Mail* published a picture of him doing this. The police watched him closely, but he did not seem to be doing anything illegal. Petro became so conspicuous that on 11 January 1968 he appeared on an extraordinary television program, where for over an hour he was questioned by David Frost and berated by members of the studio audience, many of them well known among the youth underground. Before Petro could leave the studio that night, he was arrested for failing to keep proper records of narcotics in his possession. Released on bail the next day, Petro flew to Scotland. To rescue his stranded patients, an emergency clinic was set up by volunteers at St. Anne, Soho. About a hundred addicts came in that weekend. Many of them were referred to St. Anne by Spear of the Home Office, to whom they had first turned. The newspaper publicity about the clinic at St. Anne put great pressure on the Ministry of Health to get the promised treatment centers functioning. On May 31, John Petro was struck off the Medical Register, though he appealed the action and continued to practice until he lost the appeal at the end of the year. I was told that Petro, a broken old man, could until recently be found sometimes in the men's room of the

Piccadilly Circus station, tending the sores of young addicts. Pitiable though these two men now are, they did great damage. As the day approached when the law said they would no longer be able to prescribe heroin or cocaine, first Petro and then Swan began switching their young addicts to Methedrine, which is methylamphetamine in solution, packed in sterile ampoules for injection, and which will cause manic exhilaration; users in England as in the States call it "speed" and describe its effect as that of cocaine intensified. Adolescents who were already taking amphetamine pills also switched to injecting Methedrine, which they got from friends or from Swan or Petro; many of those later became heroin addicts—the one *prima-facie* case of drug progression, though some would argue that in *that* morbid sequence, heroin is de-escalation. At the beginning of 1968, the first drug clinics were opening, in temporary quarters, with inexperienced staff. Compulsory notification of new cases was to begin February 22. Prescribing of heroin and cocaine by general practitioners was to stop on April 16. Nobody in England then would have claimed to know how many heroin addicts there really were, or whether they would come to the clinics, or how the young would start combining their drugs next.

In the midst of the confusion, haste, and apprehension, a few people were asking what the fundamental aim of the treatment centers was to be. In the summer of 1967, Griffith Edwards wrote an article for *The British Medical Journal,* which he titled "Relevance of American Experience of Narcotic Addiction to the British Scene." Dr. Edwards began:

The United States has had a large drug addiction problem for a long time. In comparison the problem in Britain seems small, but the concern here must be not so much with the problem's present absolute size as with its rate of growth . . . extrapolation to ten

years hence suggesting a quite frightening figure. In planning our
own response to this problem it is natural to turn for guidance to
America's much greater experience.

But is American experience relevant to our own country's problem? The gross disparity, diminishing though that gap may be,
between the two prevalence rates immediately suggests that different processes may be at work. One obvious explanation for this
disparity in addiction rates is the contrasting general level of social
disturbance in the two countries, as shown by the Table.

SOME INDICES OF SOCIAL PROBLEMS IN U.S.A.
AND ENGLAND AND WALES, 1964

	U.S.A.	England & Wales
Infant mortality (deaths under 1 year of age per thousand live births)	44.0	19.9
Illegitimate live births per thousand live births	121	72
Divorces granted during year per thousand population	2.3 (provisional figure)	0.7
Suicide per thousand deaths	12.0	10.4
* Murder per million population	48	6
* Robbery per million population	582	83.5 (incl. blackmail)

Data gathered from *Vital Statistics—Statistical Abstracts of U.S.A.* and
Annual Abstract of Statistics, Central Statistical Office, H.M.S.O., London.
  * For difficulties of comparison between criminal statistics of different
countries, see *Cultural Factors in Delinquency,* edited by T. C. N. Gib-
bens and R. H. Ahrenfeldt, p. 87. Tavistock Publications, London, 1966.

Edwards then presented a dry, spare table, "Some Indices of
Social Problems," to show that, compared to England, America had not only more drug addiction but two-thirds more
illegitimate births per thousand, over twice the infant-mortal-

ity rate, a divorce rate almost three and a half times as great, seven times as many robberies per million people (even counting the English weakness for blackmail), and eight times as many murders. The history of American efforts to control heroin, Edwards thought, suggested warnings: that addiction is rooted in social stress, that drug use can change unpredictably and with bewildering speed, that treatment is difficult without compulsory detention of the addict, but that "vindictive legislation" is no preventive. He wrote:

The important lesson for Britain is that, despite more than 40 years of punishing the addict, America still has a large drug-addiction rate, a well-established black market, and an addict population which is forced into varieties of criminality. . . .

The growing rate of drug addiction in Britain has forced revision of the law, but the underlying philosophy which guides the British approach remains unaltered: the thesis was and is that the interests of treatment and prevention are best served by regarding the addict as a patient, by giving him heroin if he so demands, by wooing him rather than coercing him into treatment, and by keeping addiction above ground rather than by driving it into the criminal underworld. The next few years will show whether this philosophy can be the basis of a viable policy. There is nothing in the American experience which guarantees failure, but much to suggest that we are playing against long odds—heroin is a bad and unpleasant drug for maintenance, and to hope that without any form of coercion the addict can be persuaded to abandon freely available narcotics is ambitious indeed. The whole of American experience would suggest that if our new programme is to be other than foredoomed to failure and a prelude to debacle, it must be conducted with vigour and energy, must be a matter of reaching out rather than of sitting back in hospitals, must focus on human needs and rehabilitation rather than on drug maintenance or detoxification.

In the years since the clinics opened, Edwards has continued to wonder whether—given the gross disproportions between America and Britain in so many measures of social disturbance —there is anything at all that either country can learn about drug addiction from the other. He came back to the question again in April 1973, addressing a conference called by the Royal Society of Medicine that brought several hundred British and American specialists to London. "William James even suggested that the temperament of the 'bottled lightning' American differed inexorably from that of the typical Englishman with his 'dull look and codfish eyes,'" Edwards said in his talk. Should the Americans simply give the latest data on methadone, the British merely say something about their clinics, everyone "guard against extrapolation like the plague, and then let's all sensibly go home our separate ways?" Edwards asked, and he answered, "Let us, rather, totally reject that sensible conclusion! As regards the ultimate aspects of the drug problem, America and Britain are facing absolutely identical concerns. The fundamentals are common," he said: myths and comfortable assumptions about the causes of addiction, the problem of whether to respond to the addict as sick or as bad, the question of personal liberty, the issue of the worth of the legal remedy. And most fundamental of all, Dr. Edwards said, "The touchstone for all our policies must be *cui bono? For whose good* do we legislate, criminalize, open another clinic, issue another report, mount another television spectacular, lecture at that class of school children, engage in all our actions, hold to our assumptions? Can the assumed *good* be demonstrated? *Cui bono?* The medical voice is too timid if it does not ask that question. Whether our skyline includes the Empire State Building, 1,250 feet tall, or the spire of Salisbury Cathedral, 404 feet, that question remains the same."

2

Now: Research and Practice at the English Addiction-Treatment Clinics

Lessons of profound interest are to be drawn from the British experience in combating epidemic heroin addiction, I think, but to specialists deep in the debate over the next steps in American narcotics policy those lessons are of a peculiarly frustrating kind. The experience of the British has sprung from the premise they have maintained for fifty years: that heroin (like morphine, codeine, and other opiates) has a legitimate place in medicine—primarily as a powerful analgesic, which any doctor may lawfully prescribe for his patients as his judgment dictates, but also as a tool in the management of addiction, which the British view as a medical responsibility even when an addict seems to need maintenance on regular minimum doses of heroin for months or years. When the outbreak of heroin addiction began in England in the early 1960s, fueled by a gray market in heroin prescribed to addicts legally but with lunatic generosity by a dozen or so general practitioners, it touched off considerable alarm. The British government and the medical profession reacted not by banning heroin in gen-

eral medicine, but by deciding that addicts are a unique sort
of patient who can no longer get heroin prescribed by general
practitioners; instead, addicts must now report to treatment
clinics for their heroin prescriptions. The British like to view
the clinics as no more than a modification of their long-term
medical approach to heroin and addiction, but since the clinics
opened, the growth of addiction has slowed markedly, so that,
although it is not wiped out, it seems by any standards normally applied to public-health problems to be contained.
Therefore, the natural urge is to invoke the British experience
with lawful heroin to settle immediate American policy issues—
which may explain why that experience has regularly been
misunderstood and misrepresented by both sides of the American debate. Some Americans advocate that the United States
should experiment with allowing addicts to have heroin legally.
Others propose, on the contrary, that the United States should
expand existing programs that treat heroin addicts by long
terms of compulsory hospitalization, and that this should be
done through the legal process known as civil commitment—
which would amount to treating addicts the way psychotics
were treated before tranquilizers and related drugs revolu-
tionized psychiatric care. These two extremes define the axis
along which the dispute over American policy will move in the
next several years. The dispute will grow more strident as the
chief present treatments—the varieties of methadone maintenance and abstinent therapeutic communities—come closer to
enrolling all the addicts who will volunteer for them, while
leaving many addicts, perhaps a majority, untreated. There
are already signs that this is happening: by the beginning of
1973, in several cities, including New York and Washington,
the long waiting lists for methadone programs had shortened
dramatically. But the lessons to be learned from the British approach to heroin cut crazily across the grain of the immediate

American debate. Even the success of the British approach raises problems in applying its lessons to America, for the British have incomparably fewer addicts to deal with, and even today only a small and unorganized illicit market. The United States may yet come to heroin maintenance for addicts. The legalizing of abortion suggests how suddenly the weather can change. But if we do turn to lawful heroin for addicts, the reason cannot be that we have learned from the British success anything so simple and gratifying as that their methods would work in an American setting.

Of the lessons that Americans can legitimately draw from the British experience, the first and most salutary are lessons of doubt. Heroin swirls in myth. Addicts share myths about heroin that enslave their behavior more than the pharmacology of the chemical itself: abrupt withdrawal is an agony carrying the risk of death; once hooked, always hooked; you can't understand a junkie unless you've been one. Doctors, sociologists, policemen, social workers, science writers, and bureaucrats who deal with addicts share powerful myths about heroin, too, some of which they have learned from the addicts, and in the nature of the case it is often difficult to break down the amalgam of truth and error that makes these professional misconceptions so durable. The dialogue, insofar as there has been one, between British and Americans working in drugs has been particularly useful in exposing such misconceptions. This dialogue began to be widely audible in the United States in the mid-'60s, when the English recognized their own problem, and has grown in volume since their clinics began functioning. For one thing, the clinics provide a frame, unrivaled elsewhere, for research into heroin addiction. Their clients are not merely a good sample but nearly all the addicts there are in Britain— or so I have become convinced. The numbers are manageable. The records have been kept. The addicts are known personally.

There is nowhere in British addiction research or control the vast blank space that is at the center of the drug map of any large American city. The greatest disappointment is that only in the last couple of years have the English begun to explore the most interesting ideas for research—such as what makes the difference between addicts and nonaddicts from the same background, and which methods of treatment work best. But the lessons of clinic practice are as valuable as research. From the beginning, clinic staffs have been learning how to prescribe to addicts, what psychiatric and social services are necessary, what progress toward getting addicts off drugs is possible, and what these things cost. They have been learning these things not just with a relatively tractable, relatively well-motivated sample, such as the volunteers for methadone or for abstinent communities in the United States, but—once again—with nearly all the addicts there are in Britain. In six years, ideas have evolved, sometimes surprisingly, and diverged. Researchers, clinic staffs, and civil servants are by no means unanimous on such fundamental issues as whether an addict can be stabilized on heroin over any length of time, whether methadone is a better drug for addicts than heroin, whether many heroin addicts are able to hold employment, whether many can successfully quit drugs, whether, despite the clinics, the small black market in heroin and other drugs is a danger, or whether heroin addiction in Britain will reëmerge as an explosive social problem. The divergences of English clinic practice and opinion also have salutary lessons for Americans—lessons of doubt.

Surely the myth most deeply rooted in the rock of American experience is the one about the extreme pleasure heroin gives, the ease of becoming addicted, and the agony of withdrawal. Addicts and the general public the world around, and many doctors in the United States, believe that the truly addicted who are abruptly deprived of drugs will experience severe distress from purely physical causes. The effects of withdrawal have hardly seemed open to question. Much of the original research on withdrawal was done at the United States Public Health Service Hospital in Lexington, Kentucky, in the 1930s. There various scales were drawn up that, with portentous scientific precision, graded the signs and symptoms of sudden abstinence from narcotics as ranging from mild, including yawning, lacrimation, rhinorrhea (runny nose), and diaphoresis (sweating), through moderate, with tremor, gooseflesh, anorexia (loss of appetite), abdominal cramps, and mydriasis (dilated pupils), marked restlessness and insomnia, increased respiration, and higher blood pressure, all the way to severe, with vomiting, diarrhea, priapism or return of menstrual flow, and weight loss of five pounds or more in twenty-four hours. In one version or another, the Lexington scales are still quoted, often in the tell-tale original jargon, in medical textbooks. Yet as a practical matter, the relation between signs and symptoms of withdrawal and degree of addiction is peculiarly hard to determine. Though urine tests can tell the fact of narcotic use, no test exists that can tell the quantity. The English clinics bear out what anyone who deals with addicts would expect—that even in the most familiar, least coercive settings addicts will lie about the combinations and amounts of drugs they take and the distress they feel without them. Some addicts can fake withdrawal with great skill. To complicate the problem further, heroin in the United States varies so widely in adulteration that not even the addict can really know the severity of his addiction. He reckons it in dollars. The fact remains that many American doctors have seen addicts go through extreme and degrading displays of withdrawal distress.

English heroin addicts reckon their habits in ten-milligram pills, and there is no question that they have averaged far higher daily doses than American addicts can afford. In England, a few addicts, whose habits have been established for more than a decade and who are now attending clinics, are injecting six grains or more a day, 360 milligrams; a grain a day, or six pills, is cited by clinic doctors as typical of addicts getting any heroin at all. Despite such quantities, English doctors are skeptical about the demon of withdrawal. They can't doubt that it terrifies their addicts. They don't question the need, when taking someone off narcotics, to use a stepwise reduction of doses, possibly masked for the time by tranquilizers or barbiturates. But they do suspect that the symptoms of withdrawal and their severity are elaborated from a slender physical basis by a robust mixture of conditioning and self-delusion. English doctors working with addicts say they have never or only very rarely witnessed a bad case of withdrawal.

Most telling is the evidence from prisons. The ranking expert on this is Ian Pierce James, a forensic psychiatrist, who in the years of the changeover to drug clinics was medical officer at Brixton Prison, in south London. Brixton houses adult men. Because they include prisoners freshly arrested and arraigned and sent there from all over southeast England to await trial, Dr. Pierce James saw the raw realities of all kinds of drug addiction. He now teaches at the University of Bristol and treats addicts as inpatients at Bristol's Glenside Hospital. On a ringingly bright West Country morning he picked me up at the new railway station outside Bristol. Dark, of middle height, heavy-set, and infectiously confident, Pierce James can shatter a preconception about drug addiction with practically every sentence, as I discovered as soon as we had settled into his car. There are very few addicts in Bristol, he said—until the end of 1971, only two, to his knowledge. But then, in just six months, there had been at least ten amateurish thefts of narcotics from pharmacies in Bristol suburbs; a little later, one or two at a time, eleven new addicts had surfaced, all in their early twenties or their teens, all close kin or friends. "These are unusual in that none had first been turned on in London," Pierce James said. "They stole heroin, tincture of morphine, even Nepenthe—that's an injectable narcotic for children. They tried them all. But I would think that, of the eleven, perhaps two or three were in any way really addicted. You may say this mini-demic is very alarming, but in fact a fair proportion of the stolen drugs was recovered, and no illegally imported heroin has been seized from these addicts. They were certainly not buying on any black market.

"We're hard-liners about heroin in Bristol. Any addict who presents himself to hospital will be taken in straightaway for gradual withdrawal. Or he may be put on oral methadone, as in the States. But no injectable narcotics for addicts. People tend to stress the differences between heroin and the other drugs, like alcohol, but the similarities are far greater. And nobody would think of prescribing a bottle of gin fortified with vitamin B_1 to an alcoholic every day. I'm taking you to Bristol Prison—that all right? I've got an office there; I'm a part-time forensic consultant."

We pulled up at a gateway through the thick prison wall. Pierce James bustled into a guardroom and came back in an instant with a ring of big jailhouse keys. "This is Dr. Judson, colleague from America," he called out to a guard, who peered briefly in. We drove into a cobbled parking lot surrounded by a steel-mesh fence. "Easier to tell them you're a professional colleague than to explain about the press." Inside the prison, the air was cool, fresh, and silent. "English criminals are a lot different from American," Pierce James said as we made our way down a steel staircase. "Much more passive, on the whole." Along a dusky corridor. "In fact, now that so many English mental hospitals have changed to open, short-stay institutions, we get a certain number of men for whom prison is really an asylum from a world they can't handle." Around a corner, through a heavy door, into a large office with a steel desk, bookcases, old maps.

Addicts don't get heroin in any British prison, Pierce James said. Instead, when they arrive they are withdrawn over a period of ten days with methadone, given by mouth. "In '68, '69, and '70, at Brixton, I was seeing about two hundred fifty people with clear signs of physical dependency on heroin every year. This was about one-quarter of the known population of male addicts over twenty-one in all England. One thing about the Home Office index—if there were a large number of addicts the Home Office had missed who thus had to be getting their supplies on the black market, you'd expect them to show up in places like Brixton. And they don't. In those years at Brixton, I saw *very* few addicts who were not already on the index—fewer than ten per cent.

"The junkie culture instills a phobic dread of withdrawal. These were people who had kept themselves euphoric for months on the most powerful analgesic ever in use, until they had lost their tolerance for even the normal discomforts of life—a stiff neck, a Monday-morning dysphoria. Abrupt withdrawal is usually no worse than a very bad flu. I've seen one case—one—with really extreme withdrawal signs, spontaneous ejaculation, though even that was a withdrawal not from heroin but methadone. At Brixton, I had far more trouble from barbiturate withdrawal than from heroin. Withdrawing from barbiturates, you can get convulsions, you know." Pierce James paused, then said, "We look at addiction the wrong way round, I think. We pay so much attention to the addict, and none to the kids from the same street who never become addicted. Addiction is not easy. I suspect you have to work at it. It's not an escalation; it's an escalade, rather—a series of walls to be got over. A lot of individuals start with marijuana, but heroin is a citadel few ever get to. Why?"

That afternoon, as we were driving to the train—the honorary degree had gotten me out of prison as easily as in—Pierce James came back to the difficulty of becoming addicted. "The real question is, put it this way, why do all the people who have been exposed to alcohol not inevitably become alcoholics? Why don't we compare a group of addicts with a group who have 'failed' to become addicts?"

A study that reëxamined the physiological signs and symptoms of withdrawal—with results that upset received opinion —was carried out in 1970 at the inpatient drug-dependence unit at the Bethlem Royal Hospital. Bethlem is historically the direct descendant of the Bedlam, just north of the Roman Wall, that was London's first insane asylum as early as the end of the fourteenth century. Relocated three times, most recently in 1930, Bethlem is now an affiliate of the Maudsley Hospital, where the Addiction Research Unit is located; Bethlem now sprawls on the border of Kent, south of London, and has woods and lawns, walks, cricket fields and tennis courts—all told, more than an acre of grounds per patient. The drug-dependence unit at the Bethlem is on the top floor of a two-story building, with day facilities and separate bedrooms for twenty-one patients to be withdrawn, in two groups, isolated from each other not by the drug they take but how they take it—pill or needle. The twenty-one patients, who pay nothing, are attended by three doctors (who also treat outpatient addicts at the Maudsley), two full-time psychiatric social workers, a psychologist, a full-time occupational therapist and another half-time, and twenty-two nurses. On top of all that, the unit is directed by a consultant psychiatrist, Philip Connell, a tall man, dark-haired and sleek, suited in banker's gray; he spends six half days a week there. Since the needle ward is locked, illicit drugs could be kept out; thus Dr. Connell had a controlled setting in which to study withdrawal. "I have only once seen a patient in acute withdrawal, and that was in an ambulance," he told me one morning. "There's evidence that you can control some patients' withdrawal symptoms with an injection of water—a simple saline solution. I am *very* skeptical about physical factors being the most important element in explaining withdrawal. Addicts have this big inventory of symptoms—I wonder whether it's not a very complicated psychophysiological conditioning. For example, there is such a thing as conditioned withdrawal, where even months after an ex-addict has been completely detoxified he can show the signs of classic opiate withdrawal, triggered just by the sight of a hypodermic syringe."

Connell set up an experiment in which a small group of narcotics addicts were given "medicine"—a paper cup of syrup to drink—once every day for twenty-eight days, which they understood was the length of their withdrawal treatment. Actually, the patients were divided at random into two groups —one group withdrawn all the way by decreasing doses of methadone in their syrup in just ten days, the other taken down in twenty-one days. Connell observed the one essential procedural safeguard for all research on the effects of pharmaceuticals: he worked "double blind," which means not only that the patients did not know what their doses were but also that all the staff members were kept ignorant of what was in the paper cups they were given to hand out, so that the staff's interpretations of patient behavior would not be influenced unconsciously by knowledge of who was getting what. (At the Public Health Service Hospital in Lexington, Kentucky, in the 1930s, the work on withdrawal was not even single blind; on the contrary, as a 1938 report boasted, the patients were encouraged to watch each other, "to observe for themselves that the abstinence syndrome is not so severe as they had imagined.") At the Bethlem, Connell and his co-workers put together for each case the nurses' daily notes, the patient's own complaints, individual interviews by doctors, and a chart that showed which of the classic withdrawal signs showed up and when, so that it became possible after the end of the twenty-eight days to relate them to the true physical state of withdrawal. "You'd expect the ten-day and twenty-one-day groups to cluster differently if physical factors were paramount," Connell said. "They didn't. The most important factor in the timing and development of their withdrawal symptoms seemed to be the nearness of the twenty-eighth day and complete withdrawal from 'medicine.'"

Withdrawal, however open to question, is a syndrome addicts and research psychiatrists are at least able to talk about explicitly. But at the back of that cave shimmers the question of the pleasure heroin can give, and this leaves everybody stumbling and peculiar. The myths about the delights of narcotics are compounded of dread and fascination. In the United States, they lie deep in the popular consciousness; even American doctors who work with addicts will sometimes talk about heroin with a vehemence that strikes the observer as not only exaggerated but salacious. Primary sensations in some ways beggar words, of course. What is the redness of red? Why is sweetness pleasant? Can we hope to ask the monkey with the micro-electrode in his thalamus to type a sonnet about just why he presses the lever in his cage? Yet the pleasure of narcotics, for those who get any, must be complex—and not absolute, like a primary sensation. In the prevailing incoherence, one of the earliest descriptions still stands as one of the most persuasive. In 1700, a London physician, John Jones, wrote, in a book titled *The Mysteries of Opium Revealed*:

> *It causes a most agreeable, pleasant, and charming Sensation about the Region of the Stomach*, which if one lies, or sits still, diffuses it self in a kind of *indefinite manner*, seizing one not unlike the gentle sweet *Deliquium* that we find upon our entrance into a most agreeable *Slumber*, which, upon yielding to it, generally ends in *Sleep:* But if the Person keeps himself in *Action, Discourse*, or *Business*, it seems . . . like a most delicious and extraordinary *Refreshment* of the Spirits upon very *good News*, or any other great cause of *Joy*, as the sight of a dearly beloved Person, *& c.* thought to have been lost at *Sea.* . . .
>
> It has been compar'd (not without good cause) to a permanent gentle *Degree* of that Pleasure, which Modesty forbids the naming of.

When the opiate is heroin, taken intravenously, some addicts claim that all those sensations are luridly intense. In the early weeks of addiction, or for some established addicts with a sharply increased dose, there is reported to be a bursting euphoria in the first seconds after injection—a rush that is described as though any sexual comparisons were inadequate. No English specialist denies the extreme seductiveness of heroin for many people. It really is an addictive drug. What they question is how the fact gets amplified—by credulity, loathing, or fear of temptation—into myth. Thus, an American doctor of great experience in the New York City addiction programs, visiting the London clinics, once said to me earnestly, "From what people tell me, it's just so goddam great, it's the most magnificent feeling in the whole world, it beats orgasm, it just beats anything." From the perspective of professionals working in the world of London drug addicts, that sounds as though mythmaking were salted with prurience.

Not everybody finds pleasure in heroin, as the English are in a position to know more clearly than most Americans. Addicts on a stabilized dose get no more than the prevention of withdrawal symptoms (of which even the slightest will, of course, trigger a powerful conditioned urge to find relief with the drug: ask any cigarette smoker) and some tranquilizing of anxiety. Nonaddicts given heroin for analgesia in England often dislike its dissociating, deadening power. "When they gave it to me when I had a coronary, I asked them to stop it, because I didn't like its effects," a psychiatrist told me. "I preferred a certain amount of pain." If it were not for the myth of the one shot of heroin, it would be easier to see that many factors ought to contribute in varying degrees to addiction: the drug, the body and mind of the person taking the drug, his attitudes and expectations, and the immediate circumstances, for there is a great difference in the risk of addiction between a drug experienced in a hospital bed with doctor attending and the same drug taken in the back room of a derelict house with agemates. In 1968, in an experiment lasting a fortnight, two British medical investigators took heroin regularly and became physiologically addicted; one of them, Ian Oswald, kept a diary and later published some of it in *The British Medical Journal*—an account that ought to be set next to Dr. Jones' classic description. Dr. Oswald wrote:

We've been on heroin a week now, Stuart and I. Seven days of voluntary illness. And how ill we feel. All to settle a theoretical point. . . . My personal view at present is just one made grey and utterly grim by heroin. The extraordinary thing is that it brings no joy, no pleasure. Weariness, above all. At most, some hours of disinterest—the world passing by while you just feel untouched. Even after the injection there is no sort of a thrill, no mind-expansion nonsense, no orgastic heights, no Kubla Khan. A feeling of oppressed breathing, a slight flush, a sense of strange unease, almost fear unknown. Amid all the paraphernalia, iron-maiden contraption for fore-arm blood flow, E.C.G. and skin conductance leads, face mask and valves that go clip-clop as you breathe in, out, in, out. . . . That's taken over an hour. Unsteady and uneasy you walk to the door and down the stairs. Stand and stand, trying to micturate; eventually in a series of brief spasms succeeding. Into bed and the cold sheets set off an uncontrollable shivering and chattering of teeth, fingers blanched white. All the E.E.G. wires connected properly? The inter-com switch on? . . . You doze, see a daft scene where someone throws something, jump with a sort of panic, and doze again. Hypnagogic hallucinations, they're called. Itching and itching, you scratch and turn. Why should people take this stuff—not for joy. Only for an hour of sudden shafts of panic and itching?

. . . Now it's sixteen hours since the last injection. Withdrawal symptoms are not bad, merely noticeable. The ever-present feeling of weariness just that much worse. A headache, yawning, shiverings and cold feelings, a nose that feels like a common cold, yawning again, hands a little shaky and poor in grip. . . . Never do this again.

. . . It's a month now since we stopped the stuff, though some measurements continue. It's been wonderful to feel fit and to relish life again. . . . I've thought more about a speaker from New York who was at a drug-dependence symposium earlier in the year—a sociologist, I think. He claimed it wasn't the withdrawal symptoms or the inner pleasures that kept men on heroin, but social pressure to belong with those who had taken this famously traditional exit. I'd thought him just ignorant of neuropharmacology and physiology. Now I suspect the greater ignorance was mine.

Certainly, not every youth who tries heroin for pleasure enjoys it enough to become an addict. The possibility that in the United States there are tens of thousands of occasional users of heroin, not addicted, has sometimes been raised, and obviously could make an important difference in attitudes toward addiction and in plans for its control. But under American

conditions—with heroin, so to speak, widely available except
to investigators—research into occasional users would be difficult and its meaning debatable, for many American specialists
automatically consign all such users to the ranks of what they
call pre-addicts. In this way, fear of the omnipotent seductiveness of heroin affects the very definition of the addict; he is
grossly simplified, from the man who has acquired an overpowering desire for the drug's continuance to anybody who
has tried it once. (In form—and in ambiguity of motive as well
—the error must be classed with the temperance definition of
the alcoholic or the hypermasculine definition of the homo-
sexual.) The result is circular. The way an addict is defined
determines how many addicts will be found; and simplified
definitions that inflate the numbers reduce the apparent chance
for success of any treatment plan.

The English, now that the clinics are more than six years
old, have evidence that is beginning to be suggestive about
sociological questions like why some of those who try heroin
don't persist—Dr. Pierce James' "failed addicts"—and they have
amassed a great deal of information about the ones who do
become addicted. A basic source is still the index of all known
addicts that the Home Office has kept for over forty years.
Since the clinics were established, the Home Office has shared
responsibility for the handling of addiction with the Department of Health and Social Security (formerly the Ministry of
Health), that being the ultimate fount of staff and funds for
treatment institutions of all kinds; separately from the Home
Office index, the Department of Health has kept its own, more
detailed records of addicts. (Surveying the shelf where stood
the black loose-leaf binders containing an up-to-date case
history of every addict who has ever been to a British clinic,
a Department of Health statistician said, "Nobody has a record
of this kind anywhere else in the world." With unconscious

heartlessness, he added, "Quite a nice size for statistical analysis.") Certain facts are established, if not always explained. In England, as in America, heroin addiction is primarily a disorder of young men. In the mid-'60s, it was clear from the Home Office index that the several thousand new addicts who made up the English heroin epidemic of those years were almost all in their late teens or early twenties. Indeed, English addicts tended to be even younger than American ones.

None of this has changed since then. The most recent study, an important five-year investigation being carried out by Herbert Blumberg, David Hawks, and a team of physicians and sociologists at the Addiction Research Unit, has begun by considering all the addicts showing up for the first time at all the London clinics in the course of twelve months, and has found that more than a quarter were in their late teens, that the average age was twenty-one years and eight months, and that only two per cent were thirty years old or more. There are some instructive contrasts to the United States: addicts in England are drawn quite evenly from the several social classes, and average about the same levels of education as the general populace, while black addicts, as they have always been, are disproportionately few. It continues to be true that English addicts are likely to use not just one drug but almost anything available, and almost at random—heroin, methadone, amphetamines and barbiturates, tranquilizers, cannabis, alcohol. This situation, too, is instructive. In the last two years in the United States, such multiple drug use, though once rare among adolescents who were experimenting with heroin, has been growing rapidly. Moving beyond these elementary descriptions, results tabulated in that investigation by the Addiction Research Unit show that a startling number—30 per cent—of the people who turn up once at a clinic (usually with enough evidence of narcotic addiction to require notification to the

Home Office) never come back again. Several of the recent studies agree on a related surprise: that a long time elapses, on the average, between a youth's first injections of a narcotic and his first appearance at a clinic. The lag averages two years from the time of first regular use of intravenous narcotics, by Department of Health statistics. According to the investigation by the team at the Addiction Research Unit, at least half of those who have recently come to a clinic had injected an opiate for the first time three years earlier, and had begun injecting opiates *regularly* ("daily for at least seven days" was the interviewers' phrase) two years before they approached a clinic. Such recent findings hardly upset the weight of evidence that the British approach has so far been generally successful in containing addiction. Yet they are puzzling. To solve the puzzle, researchers are beginning now to examine more closely the patterns of drug use among the young. Clinic staffs, of course, see these patterns daily, and though their impressions are partial and not rigorous they offer some leads. Staffs say, from their dealings with the one-time visitors and with their regulars as well, that many hundreds of people may have experimented with narcotics without progressing to addiction—or at least, not yet. This impression is confirmed by a very different witness, who speaks with unusual authority among adolescents in England. Don Aitken, a thin and watchful man with hair to his shoulders, is one of the present leaders of Release, a do-it-yourself legal-aid and social-welfare unit set up by youthful activists in the mid-'60s; Release has outlived the rest of the alternative society in London, and is perceived by young England—even by many of the most rebellious youths taking drugs—to be their own organization. In a recent conversation, Aitken made several laconic criticisms of the drug-treatment clinics, but then said, "One thing we have always believed is that there are a lot of occasional users of heroin—possibly as many as there are addicts. Mostly the ones who try it two or three times and then quit. But some take it every weekend for years." Despite the evident importance, for the very definition of addiction, of the possibility that some people use heroin just occasionally, almost no formal research has been done on the subject either in England or the United States; in view of the volume of research about drug addiction that does get published, this idea must be very alien to the ruling myths about heroin. So far as I know, just one preliminary paper has appeared, an American pilot study by Douglas H. Powell, published in April 1973. Powell works for the University Health Services at Harvard; but he canvassed the drug clinics, medical services, and various community mental-health centers throughout the Boston area, and asked people who had done research in addiction, without finding a single lead to somebody who used heroin only occasionally. So he put ads in two weekly newspapers, read by the young, inviting phone calls from "chippers who want to take part in a psychological study." He got nearly a hundred calls. Most of the callers had no idea that a chipper, in addict slang, is an occasional user of heroin. About thirty-five of the calls came from people who did use heroin. Among these or their friends, Powell was able to find twelve who met his criteria: somebody who has used heroin occasionally for three years or more, but who "has never had a habit or sought treatment." He interviewed and tested his twelve intensively. He found them for the most part middle class, in their early twenties, intelligent, pleasant to talk to, highly anxious, somewhat immature and irresponsible; he included in his twelve at least two who from their thumbnail case histories are on their way to true addiction; he found that all twelve were controlling their heroin use with great care, were not involved with the addict community or way of life, and had few friends who use heroin. But, as he recognized, his group was too small to permit any firm conclusion—except the most important conclusion of all, that occasional heroin users are not rare. Some English doctors go further (as do some Americans) and suggest that it is actually hard for the average youth to become an addict.

The availability of the clinics and their captive clientele make possible research projects designed to penetrate the causes of addiction. Yet the questions are genuinely difficult. Addicts make unreliable witnesses, with poor and self-serving memories; the drugs they take are almost sure to have altered precisely the social behavior and personality traits that are at issue. Thus, any research, wherever carried out, that looks retrospectively into the biographies of addicts begins with grave problems. An alternative is to work forward in time; that is, to start with a group of addicts today—or, ideally, with a very much larger and younger group in which nobody is yet using drugs—and follow all its members for years in order to see what happens to them and how their fates might have been predicted. Research like that is easier in England than in America, but it is expensive anywhere, and obviously takes a great deal of time. English studies along such lines have only recently begun. Most are being done by the Addiction Research Unit, where they are designed with an intellectual elegance that is the mark of the unit's director, Griffith Edwards. Some of the most important projects will not be completed for years.

What has emerged provisionally is a social psychology of drug use, a picture of experimentation by youth in small, mutually reinforcing groups or subgroups of friends. Several things about the groups are clear enough: for one, the repeated availability of a drug or the presence of a syringe does have an effect; for another, an addict is very rarely given his first injection by a stranger—the myth of the malign pusher is

another to be deflated. The decision to take drugs may hinge
on almost accidental factors, but, perhaps unexpectedly, it
often seems to be a deliberate choice—though a choice not just
of a drug but of a role or a relationship. If a young man is
using many different drugs, getting them from friends or
through a number of small-scale black-market sources, he may
avoid going to the clinics because they offer only methadone
and heroin; or because he has heard that the clinics don't
prescribe enough to satisfy him; or because he doesn't want to
admit he's hooked; or because he doesn't want to be involved
with authorities, regular appointments, and so on. It is also
clear that within the youth subgroups, drug taking and even
outright addiction are seen very differently from the way they
are elsewhere in the society. Drug use may be recognized in
such a group as, so to speak, an accepted way to be deviant—
giving the users a recognized role to play—or the users may not
feel deviant or "sick" at all, but normal and right. These small
groups of addicts are obviously fluid in membership, and may
differ from one to another: compare the middle-class adolescents in the West End in the late '60s, who even saw themselves as disturbed, to the working-class addicts of the East
End, who seemed to clinic psychiatrists to be quite typical of
their community. Yet the suggestion is that within all the
various groups there must be much the same patterns of inter-
play by which behavior—including drug taking—is chosen and
reinforced. Such group interactions, the argument runs, produced the addicts who came to be seen as typical, in three
essential respects, of the epidemic: they were very young;
they were not stable socially, not able to keep a good hold on
their daily lives; and they infected others. In these respects
they were the opposite of the addicts who had been familiar
to the members of the Rolleston Committee. "Dr. Rolleston's
prescription was for a very different illness," Griffith Edwards

said. There were still addicts around who would have been recognizable to Rolleston: in 1967, for example, the Home Office knew of several doctors quietly taking morphine, and of 313 addicts of a variety of narcotics, including nine on heroin, whose addiction had originated in the course of treatment for something else. These types were no more trouble than they had ever been. But were there any of the new English heroin addicts who were not part of the conspicuous, infectious, degenerating youthful groups? Was the concept of the stable addict useful any longer? In 1970, Gerry Stimson and Alan Ogborne, who were then working at the Addiction Research Unit, published the results of a survey they had made of addicts getting heroin at treatment clinics in London; Dr. Stimson has since developed the results into a book. Stimson and Ogborne covered all but one of the clinics in London, and got in touch with a sample, chosen at random, of 111 addicts, which was just over one-third of all addicts in London then receiving heroin by clinic prescription. Their average interview lasted an hour and forty minutes. They turned up some interesting facts along the way: 39 per cent of the addicts said they were employed full time, and 24 per cent had indeed worked the full previous week; 84 per cent reported that in the month before the interview they had used drugs not prescribed for them at the clinic; 34 per cent said that in the previous three months they had committed some criminal act, not counting violations of drugs laws. The aim of the study was to find out how addicts differ. To get at this, Stimson analyzed the mass of interview information, and found four fundamental characteristics by which the addicts could be measured: regularity of employment, irregularity of sources of income, criminal activities, and contact or involvement with other addicts. The seventy-six men in the sample, when rated on these characteristics, clustered into four very different types. Stimson called them the stable, the junkies, the loners, and the two-worlders. The stable addicts had the highest employment scores, and the least irregularity of income, the least criminal activity, the least involvement with other addicts. The junkies were the opposite of the stable in all four variables. The loners had employment records nearly as bad as the junkies', but were not particularly criminal nor in touch with other addicts. The two-worlders were nearly as regular in employment and sources of income as the stable addicts, yet were involved with other addicts and in crime almost to the same degree as the junkies. Many other characteristics of the addicts emerged in relation to Stimson's basic four-way classification. For example, junkies were the ones most likely to have shared a syringe with a friend last week, or to have prepared an injection using the water from the bowl of a public toilet, or to have injected themselves in a public place like a telephone booth or a shop doorway. Stimson's stable addicts, on the other hand, really seemed to have their lives organized. They were being prescribed more heroin than the junkies and were the least likely to be using other drugs; they slept far more regularly, ate far more regularly, reported that they were able to work even though taking heroin, and so on. When all the addicts were followed up a year later, the stable addicts were the ones whose lives had changed least. And though the junkies were conspicuous, in point of fact they were heavily outnumbered by the stable addicts in the sample: thirteen to twenty-five.

So far, such a social psychology of drug use generally agrees with explanations that have been offered by a number of thoughtful people in the United States; there has been a lively transatlantic traffic in such ideas during the past five years. English investigators are naturally trying to push them further, though the effort soon runs ahead of research evidence yet available. Meanwhile, results that should be among the most useful are promised by several studies conceived more narrowly. Some are trying, reflexively, to uncover the attitudes and prescribing policies of clinic staffs, and what effects these have on addicts. Others aim to get the first objective evidence, where possible through double-blind studies, about which drugs and treatment approaches work best for different sorts of addicts.

In the winter of 1967–68, as the drug-dependence clinics were organized and began to open, research was far from the minds of their staffs. Their entire energies went to curbing chaos and incipient panic—their own as well as the addicts'. The addicts were wildly excited by the drugs they were taking, the life they were leading, and the public controversy they had attracted; beneath the excitement, they were apprehensive about what the clinics would do to them. The clinic staffs were almost entirely inexperienced in the work, they had almost no guidelines, and they, too, had little idea of what to expect. The law was clear but brief. Compulsory notification of new cases was to begin February 22. After April 16, to prescribe heroin or cocaine to an addict would require that the doctor have a special license from the Home Office. What the government had arranged with the senior consultant physicians, who largely run the British medical profession, was a plan that shifted responsibility for maintaining addicts from general practitioners in their surgeries to psychiatrists at the clinics. Several of the general practitioners who had been working with addicts applied to the Home Office, but not one has ever been issued a license. The rare general practitioner who wants to work with addicts now has few tools, though he can still prescribe methadone.

The treatment of addicts had always ranked low in British

medicine; given the never-ending importunities of these patients, and their dubious prognosis, their unpopularity is under-
standable, but it was also one reason their care had been left
so long and with so little support to the few doctors who had
been willing to take them on. The change to drug-dependence
clinics gave the work only slightly more prestige. Fourteen
outpatient heroin clinics were decreed for London. Other treatment centers were later set up in provincial cities, from Belfast
and Glasgow to Brighton, but these are much smaller than the
ones in London, and not all take outpatients. Each clinic in
London was attached to one of the teaching hospitals there.
British teaching hospitals, though nominally responsible to the
Department of Health, are powerful princedoms. Being independent of regional hospital boards, they could be given
money directly by the department and then make their own
decisions about housing and staffing the clinics, and, as it
turned out, about almost every other aspect of policy and
treatment as well. Though American visitors often find it hard
to believe, there is no central direction or administration of the
clinics.

Several clinic psychiatrists also pointed out to me that
British psychiatry is different from American in ways that
affect one's understanding of the clinics. It is less highly regarded, and does not have the strong intellectual tradition that
supports it in the United States. Its practices, out of which the
drug clinics evolved, are those of a cadet branch of physical
medicine. Among the consultant psychiatrists in 1968, perhaps
a majority were extremely uncomfortable about the idea of
maintaining addicts with heroin, and many protested that their
profession was being forced into unethical conduct just to
solve a Home Office problem, the *police* problem, of preventing the growth of an illicit market. Yet there were ironies. To
possess one of the new Home Office licenses to prescribe to

addicts became, instantly, a mark of status among psychiatrists; some six hundred licenses were issued, many to the same men who had said categorically that they couldn't conceive of giving an addict heroin. The licenses are only now being weeded out. Most were never exercised. To recruit the staff for the new clinics, although fewer than two score doctors were needed, was not easy. With the general practitioners excluded, nobody who had any experience whatever was left, except the few consultant psychiatrists—Thomas Bewley, Philip Connell, James Willis, and a very few others—who had been working with addicts as inpatients in hospitals. These at first spread themselves over several clinics each. Virtually all the full-time members of the clinic staffs, though, were new to addiction. Some of them say even today that they were press-ganged. The low standing of the drug-treatment centers was evident, too, from the quarters they were given, which were quickly converted from other uses, and were usually cramped, tacky, and even hard to find. "We were started in the old chest clinic," I was told by Martin Mitcheson, the psychiatrist who runs the drug clinic at University College Hospital, in London. "You must understand that addiction has succeeded tuberculosis as a social disease, and you hide addicts at the backs of hospitals." Yet the shabby clinics certainly didn't seem crisp and institutional; they almost felt like part of the underground scene, and, if anything, made the addicts feel safer. "Anyway, unlike your American street junkies, our addicts have always been doctor-oriented," an English social worker told me in 1968. That winter, the addicts began to sidle and swagger into the clinics—at first mainly the wiser, middle-class, Piccadilly addicts but by spring also the half-articulate youths with their Cockney triphthongs. These were the high months in England for acting out the style of the junkie life, even if you were only sixteen and were injecting heroin only once a week. The addicts were strung out on apprehension and excitement. They were used to wheedling and bullying their general practitioners. They thought they had a legal right to heroin. They sensed their numbers and cohesiveness. The raw clinic staffs immediately faced the problems that had overwhelmed even the most responsible of their predecessors among the general practitioners who had prescribed to addicts.

The medical skills required for dealing with a heroin addict are fairly crude, the administrative precautions minimal—or they are if maintenance is the first aim and no sizable black market is competing. The new clinics did have a prototype. The city of Birmingham had already experienced its own small epidemic of heroin addiction, and this had been fought to a standstill a year or so earlier by John Owens, at All Saints' Hospital there, and his head nursing officer, Edward David Hill. Dr. Owens, a psychiatrist, had come to All Saints' in 1964 and set up a clinic chiefly to treat alcoholics, though he had expected to get an occasional more exotic case from Birmingham's large population of Pakistani and Indian immigrants. To this day, his clinic sees a number of Sikhs, older men, who have become addicted to an opium tea they brewed by steeping dried poppy heads in boiling water. They are given morphine tablets, by mouth, some as much as two grains a day. Without morphine, the Sikhs can't function. With it, they work and support families. Owens successfully withdrew his first young heroin addict, as an inpatient, in the summer of 1965. By the end of the year, he was getting two or three new cases a week. By March 1966, there were about fifty addicts in Birmingham. Owens determined to monopolize heroin there. Working with the police, the pharmacists, and the local medical association, he got everyone to agree that nobody else would prescribe to addicts.

The practices that Owens' clinic then evolved were simple.

When a new addict presented himself, Mr. Hill, the nursing officer, would take a urine sample, complete a brief questionnaire, and then examine the addict's arms. "It's not too hard to read the scars," Hill told me. "Tattooing of veins, signs of abscesses, a needle or a pin—some lads would come in, swear they were heroin addicts, and show an arm full of punctures, every one made that same day with a pin." An hour later, Owens would interview the new case. Then the addict would wait, under observation, for the results of the urinalysis. Analyses for drugs have been developed to the point where they are not difficult, just tedious and finicky. Narcotics, barbiturates, and amphetamines can all be identified, but only by running three different series of separations, while extra tests for tranquilizers and even for aspirin may be necessary. ("Poly-drugs? They'd inject salad cream!" Hill told me in Birmingham. A doctor in New York told me of an addict who once injected peanut butter.) Heroin itself breaks down to morphine in the body before it is excreted. Making a clear distinction between, say, morphine and codeine may take an additional technique. Some American laboratories are now equipped so that a single technician can test sixty urine samples that thoroughly in a working day, but when the Birmingham clinic opened, the methods available were much slower. If the tests indicated that a new addict at All Saints' had taken heroin that day, and if he was showing withdrawal signs, Hill would give him perhaps half a grain of the drug and a syringe; the way he injected the drug would indicate how experienced he was, Hill said, and the effect of the dose could be judged. Owens began by prescribing heroin to addicts weekly, but found they would use a week's supply in two days. Given three prescriptions a week, they would shoot a long weekend in a day. The clinic was soon writing prescriptions for each day. It was open several afternoons and one evening a week, and addicts were required to come in every week at an appointed time for a talk, however brief, with Owens, and a urine check. To stop prescription forgeries and to keep all the addicts from congregating at one place, Owens began introducing each addict personally to one of several selected pharmacists to whom the addict's prescriptions were thereafter mailed in weekly batches. These procedures that Owens and Hill devised have become standard clinic practice.

"So many people think the be-all and end-all of the clinic is to get them off heroin," Hill said. "We think of what we do in relation not just to the addict but the community. If we could maintain forty on heroin, and then never get another addict, we would do it. But of those original fifty that had come in by the spring of '66, to the best of our knowledge only five are still on drugs. And only two deaths. There's no reason to get the deaths. With no reason for overdoses, and with clean—even domestically clean—syringes, you don't get septicemia, and you don't get liver damage. They are more susceptible to sickness in general, it's true."

The clinic at All Saints' drew attention and many visitors. The Home Secretary then—it was the midpoint of Harold Wilson's earlier Labour government—was Roy Jenkins, who was personally committed to an energetic program of reforms, including, for example, a liberalization of the laws covering abortion and homosexuality. Jenkins visited the Birmingham clinic in the fall of 1967. "As I recall, I was very encouraged by this visit," he told me in a conversation at the House of Commons early in 1973. "I was encouraged by their evident and apparently well-grounded confidence that a clinic approach to controlled prescribing could work." That fall, Jenkins also visited the United States, to learn about the drug problem, particularly in New York City. "The American experience certainly never began to move me to consider total prohibition of heroin here," he said. "I saw a lot of people and a lot of treatment centers. The thing that struck me first and most forcibly in the United States, however, was the link—only too obvious a link—between addiction and crime. Such a link did not exist in this country, and to go out of the way to create such a link seemed self-evidently foolish. Throughout, I was firmly against criminalizing addiction, as I think we all were. What was wanted was other kinds of social controls, for the addicts under medical care and also—very importantly—for the doctors themselves. We thought that a chief objective had to be to institutionalize the care of addicts through the clinic setting, in which nobody would be acting alone but, instead, as part of a group with checks and supports for the doctors as well as the more visible controls supporting the addicts."

The difficult first months of the new clinics were described to me with remembered disquiet, even five years later, by Margaret Tripp, the psychiatrist who ran the Addiction Unit at St. Clement's Hospital, in London, for its first three and a half years. In the early months of 1968, all the new English clinics prescribed heroin with fair abundance. They had little choice, their staffs believed, if they were to prevent the growth of illicit sources of heroin and keep addicts from turning to other drugs. "As you clearly realize, our purpose at the beginning was to *seduce* the buggers," Dr. Tripp said. "But a lot of my colleagues would cheat themselves about this. When the general practitioners were prescribing heroin—ah, that was vicious. 'But when *I* give heroin, it's medical treatment.'" We talked in the kitchen of her house in Colchester, an hour east and north of London, while she fried sausages for her children's lunch and then put out cheese and fruit for us; as she worked and talked, her recollections at first seemed self-depreciatingly slangy and almost cryptic, but gradually she built up a remarkable impression of the psychological pressures and even physical dangers that clinic staffs faced in bringing a large number of addicts under control—and an impression, as well, of the stubborn and womanly integrity that kept her at it. She had trained in psychiatry "at the bin down the road," meaning the mental hospital in Colchester; in the fall of 1967 she had answered a help-wanted ad for drug clinic staffs in *The British Medical Journal.* "There was no competition for the job, needless to say! I went to St. Clement's in January. Started dishing out heroin at the end of February." The addicts in her area— St. Clement's is just off the Mile End Road, which is the Piccadilly of the Cockney East End—were drawn from a distinctively urban, working-class community with a marked criminal tradition, centuries old. She inherited most of the addicts who had been getting heroin and cocaine, and other drugs as well, from the notorious Dr. Christopher Michael Swan (he who later went mad and is now in Broadmoor). The addicts' extortionate pressures on Swan had grown so great that he turned over a block of signed prescription blanks to one young man, who sat in the doctor's surgery filling them in and collecting the fee. For about seven weeks, from the opening of St. Clement's clinic until the Home Office licensing regulation at last came into force, on April 16, Dr. Swan was still legally prescribing heroin in generous quantity, in competition with Dr. Tripp.

"Addicts have this very bent relationship with their doctor," she told me. "I had the same pressures on me in the outpatient clinic that Swan had in his surgery, and I therefore had a lot of feeling for him. He was an unfortunate and ill-used man, and when I first met him was by no means mad. He explained to me at great length and in great detail why the clinics were going to fail. At that stage, he began to see himself as the only one who understood the addicts, and as their savior. I was fortunate in being a woman. They were often wildly aggressive and threatening, but they would not actually harm a woman, though there were times I was not sure of that. Later, some of my favorite patients were the ones who had leaned on Swan, because they were the ones who were most solidly, genuinely East End. At the beginning, the addicts were ostracized by everyone else at the hospital; even the staff was ostracized. We weren't bothered at first about overprescribing, but wanted to be generous enough to net all the addicts at one go. Quite unawares, we were doing just what the government really wanted. We had over a hundred patients by May. They ranged in age from seventeen to thirty-five. Some of my older guys were taking up to fifteen grains of heroin a day. The highest I ever had was a musician, older, working regularly for the B.B.C. He took twenty grains a day. But most of my guys were around seventeen years old, and for them a *high* dose would be four or five grains." I asked her if it was possible to stabilize an addict—his dose, and his life—on heroin, and she said, "This is one of those things you don't believe in the States, isn't it? But a lot has to do with the intentions of the guy himself. Some seem insatiable; some do stabilize. I had kids in the same dull job for months—sometimes we even found ourselves wondering why they weren't more ambitious. When we got all the addicts in, we began to get the doses more nearly right; knowing the boys and their families—they were ninety per cent boys, and most were living with their families—we made fewer mistakes. After a year, perhaps half of them had stabilized their dosage." When Dr. Tripp's children had finished their lunch and gone out, she said that prescribing heroin to addicts had not been comfortable. "You know, I'll be paying for this conversation for days. It was a profound emotional experience. At first, I felt like the worst example of the Melanie Klein bad mother. I was giving these cases—and they were my patients, and they felt like my children—I was giving them this poison. I got over that, later. For the most part.

"You Americans are at the stage of calling addicts delinquent. When we started, we were calling them sick. I can see how that would look to you like a big advance. But after a time, when I knew them, I wasn't calling them anything. I gave up being a headshrinker with these guys almost immediately. It would be nice if you could profit by our mistakes. It would be nice if you could miss out the 'sick' stage altogether. The addicts themselves are against being labeled sick. The clinics force the addicts to be patients. The main reason I finally left, a year ago, was that to perpetuate my job I'd have had to create work, to go on labeling people sick who had not yet perceived themselves that way."

Margaret Tripp made me see that though the clinics were not explicitly planned in these terms, probably the most important thing they achieved was to restructure the relation between doctors and addicts. On the one side, the clinics erected an entirely new protective scaffolding around the doctors, and, on the other, they broke down many of the supple but tenacious bonds that had joined the addicts, and had lent addiction much of its strength. "This is what that entire recent lot of drugs legislation is about—not drugs at all, but getting at my profession," she said. "What do the clinics do? They save a physician from isolation: no man in isolation can hope to deal with a hundred drug addicts."

A hundred addicts is about the number actively attending a typical London drug clinic. Each is required to come in once a week; the hundred appointments are scheduled across two or three long afternoons, with one night session for those who can't get away from their jobs during the day. To deal with a hundred addicts, a clinic has the half-time services of a senior psychiatric consultant and the full time of at least one

other psychiatrist. There are also two or three nurses. Four
social workers for every hundred addicts are called for by
official standards; clinics usually have two, though some have
one more, half time. Organization on a comparable scale to
treat New York City's 150,000 true heroin addicts, or its quar-
ter-million users (if that really is how many there are), would
require over fifteen hundred clinics and, at a doctor and a half
each, nearly twenty-three hundred fully qualified psychiatrists; at the beginning of 1974, the American Psychiatric Association had 2,007 members in New York City, and the city
had 19,641 doctors of all sorts. Some four thousand nurses
would be needed, and from four to eight thousand social
workers. In London, each clinic is at a different hospital.
Within the clinic, and enveloping the clinic staff within the
hospital as a whole, there is a network of almost constant professional contacts that range upward from canteen tea breaks;
the support these contacts give was pointed out by both Roy
Jenkins and Dr. Tripp, and had been explained to me by
Martin Mitcheson, of University College Hospital. "At the
teaching hospitals, we are much more subject to our colleagues'
criticisms and unspoken controls than we would be if we were
operating an independent clinic or working anyplace that
doesn't have a structure of committee meetings and dining
clubs and so on," Mitcheson told me. "I think this is important.
And then, you see, London is a small enough drug scene so
that we *all* meet together, quite spontaneously this grew up.
Each of the various subprofessions concerned with the clinics
has a monthly meeting. The nurses meet—over wine and cheese,
I believe. The social workers meet. The doctors meet. The
secretaries don't—but you know, perhaps they should, for they
have a key role when the addict walks in the door. And then
there's the official quarterly meeting at the Department of
Health, which we all have to go to, because we're terrified

somebody else might get an extra ration of jam. Which is another control mechanism. Now, I don't think this could be done in the States, given the size of the American drug scene."

For addicts, the advent of the clinics meant a change in social relationships, too, but in the reverse direction: the cohesive youthful subgroups characteristic of addiction are now quietly discouraged and replaced in a variety of ways. "When you get a group of addicts together and talking, they reinforce each other's addiction" is an English clinic maxim. Whatever the psychiatric orientation of the clinic directors, almost all of them actively resist the therapeutic and encounter groups they see as the most conspicuous, and bizarre, feature of American rehabilitation efforts. "Oh, yes, we've watched your shouting sessions on television," Margaret Tripp said. An English clinic's waiting room will not often have as many as half a dozen people in it, counting girl friends and babies. Mailing of prescriptions directly to pharmacies, each chosen because it is near the addict's job or home, with a pickup hour set, and with no pharmacy asked to handle more than a few such prescriptions, has shut down Piccadilly and the Mile End Road as marts for addicts. Perhaps the most conspicuous change is the transformation of Boots' all-night pharmacy in Piccadilly Circus, where addicts used to wait by the dozen, edgy and shrill, as midnight approached and their next day's scripts would be negotiable. These midnights, Boots' is deserted; only about twenty addicts fill their prescriptions there now during the entire day. The temptation to flaunt junkie behavior has been greatly reduced; no small part of the British toleration of legal addiction is due to the clinics' success in getting addicts out of sight. Addicts can no longer swarm from one doctor to a new one; clinic transfers must be justified, and are now infrequent. American doctors working with drugs often seem to think that the size of a prescription written at an English clinic is set by outright bargaining between doctor and addict; Americans I have talked with don't mention poison but flinch at prescribing pleasure, and to haggle over it seems intolerably unprofessional. Haggling undoubtedly used to take place between addicts and prescribing general practitioners; it is no longer at all characteristic of English addicts' meetings with their doctors. Though practices vary somewhat, at the best-run clinics the prescriptions for the next seven days are determined and written during a weekly closed-door all-staff conference. Inescapably the prescription is what brings the addict in every week; once he is there, what he talks about with the psychiatrist and the social worker, if he is at all stable, will be his job, his housing, his parents, his girl, ordinary things—and drugs chiefly in relation to these. The concerns of the occasional female addict are often still more poignant, since she is very likely to be living with a man who is an addict, too, and may also be painfully anxious about the effects of drugs on possible children. "Many of my addicts like to pose as deliberate dropouts from the middle class," Mitcheson said at University College Hospital, "but I know them well enough by now to be sure they don't want to write a William Burroughs book. What they do want is a semidetached council house and a car." ("Most of *ours*," said John Mack, a psychiatrist at Hackney Hospital, "have already *got* a council house and a second-hand car.") Thus, the structural transformations brought about by the clinics have enabled the growth of the therapeutic essential—a relationship between doctor and addict in which both must expect that they will be working together over months and years. If the clinics have accomplished nothing more than this, they must be counted a heart-stirring success.

That was not the first and most visible accomplishment, however. The numbers were—the marked slowing of the growth of heroin addiction. It is surely one of Satan's greater strengths that in social crises the numbers make headlines, while in social victories the numbers make only statistics. But since any judgment of the clinics depends on how the statistics are viewed, they can't be left to the many who view them with prejudice. The Home Office index continued to yield several numbers, in parallel, working down from the all-inclusive total of addicts of all kinds of narcotics. In 1967, that top figure had been 1,729. Three-quarters of those, 1,299, were heroin addicts. Nine people were still counted as having acquired their addiction to heroin in the course of medical treatment for something else, usually cancer; these, if not in a hospital, were transferred to the new clinics, too, but, as a Home Office source said, "We didn't insist that a seventy-year-old come sit in the waiting room every week with the junkies." That left 1,290 heroin addicts in 1967—an apparently irreducible figure. As the clinics were being set up, the Home Office bravely maintained that the true number of narcotics addicts of all kinds could not be more than three thousand.

Through 1968, as compulsory notification and the clinics brought the addicts in, the index swelled. By the end of 1968, the year's total for all addicts known to the Home Office reached 2,782. A year later it was 99 higher, and near these levels it seems to have stabilized. Even allowing for some the index will have missed, the Home Office estimate for narcotics addicts of all kinds turned out to be essentially right—and, it is said, nobody was more surprised than the Home Office. Of the fewer than three thousand addicts, the ones that counted were the ones taking heroin—2,240 of them. Death, emigration, prison, and cure had subtracted some addicts since 1967, so the 2,240 included 1,306 new heroin cases. Thus, it looked at first glance as though the rate of increase had itself increased, which is how the English changeover was often reported in the United States. So another sturdy myth was born, for the truth seems to be that though there were indeed new addicts, the apparent size of the increase was due to the change in the way the numbers were collected—that is, the introduction of compulsory notification—combined with the very real pressure, wherever several addict friends had been dividing up a single private prescription, for them all to come to a clinic. At the end of the 1960s, no one could seriously charge that the index, newly based, was missing any vast number of heroin addicts. If it had been, these would have begun to turn up with withdrawal signs in police stations and jails, in hospital emergency and casualty wards, and in morgues. But Ian Pierce James' experience in those years at Brixton Prison, where fewer than ten per cent of the many addicts he saw were not on the index, was duplicated everywhere else. For instance, of the ninety-eight addicts who died in 1969 and 1970 only four were not known to the Drugs Branch.

Besides heroin, the clinics had methadone to work with, and when the doctor thought an addict needed a barbiturate or tranquilizer, he could prescribe it—in pills, of course. But other strong, injectable drugs were often available to addicts outside the clinics, and from time to time, unpredictably, a craze for one of these would sweep the English adolescents. The first of these to confront the clinics, in 1968, was injectable methylamphetamine. As the day approached when they could no longer give addicts heroin, two of the prescribing doctors—Petro and then Swan—had begun deliberately switching their customers to methylamphetamine, and this drug helped create the manic emotionalism among young addicts in the clinics' first year. It was marketed in thirty-milligram ampoules, almost entirely by one supplier, Burroughs Wellcome, under the trade name Methedrine. Injected repeatedly—and Pierce James warned his colleagues in a letter to *The Lancet* in April 1968 that some users were injecting ten ampoules a day—methylamphetamine produces a psychosis that had been described a decade earlier, at the Bethlem Royal Hospital, as "indistinguishable from acute or chronic paranoid schizophrenia." Though the London youth newspaper *International Times* shouted the slogan "Speed Kills," borrowed from the United States, Pierce James saw over four hundred cases of intravenous amphetamine use in Brixton Prison in 1968. That October, with inspired simplicity, the Drugs Branch and the Department of Health got Burroughs Wellcome to agree to supply Methedrine ampoules only to hospitals. The Methedrine craze was quenched literally in days; the temperature of the addict community plummeted. Observers are still surprised that the strategy worked, and baffled that no laboratories in England ever made amphetamines illegally, as laboratories in the United States and Canada do.

"The drug problem is like a huge soft balloon," an observer at the Home Office told me. "You squeeze it down hard here, and it pops up there. Usually where you weren't looking. Any tightening up or restriction you do has got to be seen in relation to the whole field of choice open to the people you're dealing with." Those who had been injecting themselves with methylamphetamine were thought likely to substitute injections made from amphetamine tablets, which was, for example, what adolescent drug takers in Sweden were doing at the time. Little of that occurred. Instead, many who had learned with methylamphetamine to be dependent on the hypodermic needle switched to heroin or to injectable methadone. By the spring of 1969, others were injecting barbiturates, which they did by crushing and then dissolving them in water and filtering the liquid through cotton wool. Intravenous barbiturates, except for a couple of briefly acting anaesthetics like Pentothal, have almost no place in medical practice; their use by adolescents is an English phenomenon almost exclusively, so far.

English doctors say that intravenous barbiturates (like methyl-amphetamine) are worse than heroin. Addicts injecting bar-biturates don't simply get euphoric and then sleepy; they become profoundly confused and unable to take care of themselves. The drug, in the way it is prepared and injected, will produce thrombophlebitis, clotted inflammations of the vein—or, if the vein is missed, abscesses that can become infected. Patients withdrawing from barbiturates are likely to go into convulsions. Through most of 1969, the sick, filthy, shambling youths on barbiturates were as noticeable in Piccadilly Circus every night as the heroin addicts once had been. "But bar-biturate injecting is self-limiting," a doctor told me grimly. "With these patients the immediate problem of treatment is to keep them alive." At that same period, youthful drug takers not compulsively attracted by the needle reverted to swallow-ing amphetamines, or, in a new fashion, sleeping pills. On 11 January 1969, a letter in *The British Medical Journal* warned of the growing popularity of a capsule with the trade name Mandrax, in which the chief ingredient is methaqualone, one of a class of nonbarbiturate hypnotics that has recently been discovered; in the United States, methaqualone appears under the trade name Quaalude. Users say methaqualone produces not only intoxication but sometimes hallucinations and am-nesia; it is still popular today in England, and by the fall of 1972 its use among adolescents had begun to grow rapidly in the United States. Another pill was Valium, from still another new class of hypnotic and depressant drugs; a large dose of Valium is hard to distinguish in its effects from alcohol. Almost any pill available was being tried, and often in combinations in which two drugs would act together to produce unpredictable and greatly intensified effects. And almost anything *was* avail-able: though the size of the illicit market should not be exag-gerated, it has of course been fed, sporadically and uncontrollably, from the lawful market, the capsules and tablets prescribed in unimaginable hundreds of millions a year by perfectly ordinary general practitioners to perfectly ordinary patients. English surveys of what doctors prescribe have shown repeatedly that these mood-changing drugs go typically to patients who are middle-aged, seventy to eighty per cent women, and in small regular amounts that suggest inescapably that a drug dependence is being maintained. The size of this lawful market would be very hard to exaggerate: in England and Wales in 1970, there were about 2,000 deaths from barbiturate poisoning, and at least 1,300 of the deaths were suicides; at the end of that year the Home Office knew of 1,175 addicts of heroin or methadone or both.

In the fall of 1968, just when the methylamphetamine problem was solved and multiple-drug use was growing, the first traces of illicitly imported heroin began to appear. Its arrival was due to no organized criminal effort and, indeed, was fortuitous; it was not intended for English addicts, and at the start few of them would touch it. Unlike the pure, safe tablets they were used to, illicit heroin in England is a brownish powder, which in recent seizures has been from ten to twenty per cent narcotic (and very low-grade narcotic at that, the morphine not fully acetylated) adulterated with caffeine and sometimes with barbiturates as well as with fillers ranging from sugar to talc. The real surprise was its source. Though France is so close to England, and has been said until recently to be the proximate source of most heroin in America, not since His Majesty's Customs seized six grams of French heroin in 1937 has there been the faintest suspicion that any important quantity was coming across the Channel. The illicit brown granules come from Hong Kong. Heroin addiction is widespread among the Chinese in Hong Kong, I was told early in

1973 by Commander Robert Huntley, of Scotland Yard, who had just been there. The rate is at least one in seventy, perhaps one in thirty. The users there rarely inject the mixture, however; instead they sprinkle it on metal foil, light a match, move the flame beneath the metal, and inhale the fumes through a drinking straw in the nostril or, when pressed, through the cover of the matchbox. They call this "chasing the dragon." Illicit heroin in England is known as "Chinese" to addicts, police, and doctors alike. One afternoon late in 1968, I was talking with a leader of the London youth underground, a beautiful ex-model named Caroline Coon—it was she who organized Release, as a twenty-four-hour-a-day legal-aid service for adolescents arrested on marijuana charges—when two of her addict friends stopped in with the news that something called Chinese heroin was on sale in the East End. The caffeine in it, they said, gave it an exotic potency. That was its first appearance among the addicts.

The explanation of the arrival and spread of Chinese heroin in England is so unlikely that before offering it my informant at the Home Office cleared his throat and looked away. "We've had in recent years, as I suppose you are aware, an explosion of Chinese restaurants in this country," he said. "With substantial immigration from the Crown Colony to staff them. What information we have points to the conclusion that there are now about fifteen Chinese users—smokers—in the Soho area. Evidently, some others in the provinces. Chinese restaurants have opened everywhere. How the contact arose between our indigenous junkies and this lot, we are not sure. One British addict told us he had been living over—or in—a billiard hall in London with some Chinese, who had this powder they said was heroin. They smoked it. He tried injecting it. It is pretty certain that the original customers among our junkies were known addicts who were supplementing their clinic supplies. Then, in August 1969, again for unexplained reasons, we just ceased to hear of Chinese heroin. Several explanations were suggested. One was that there had been two or three fatalities pretty clearly linked with Chinese H, which scared the kids off. Another was that the local Chinese themselves choked off the supply to the kids; the Chinese community is authoritarian, and possibly didn't like the police attention that was being attracted to it. But in April 1970, Chinese heroin was suddenly back on the streets. Where it has remained ever since. And it is unquestionably true that many addicts have learned to supplement their clinic drugs with Chinese heroin."

The English understand that one of their greatest protections against an invasion of drugs from Marseille is the American market's limitless appetite for heroin at high prices. In London, the black-market price of heroin—the English tablets— held steady for years at one pound a grain, or from one-twelfth to one-twentieth of New York retail prices for heroin. After the clinics opened and began to cut back overprescribing, the price slowly climbed. A packet of Chinese heroin containing about half a grain, discounting the adulterants, sold for about five pounds in the summer of 1972; by December 1973, the same money bought a quarter grain or less. Convictions for possession of illicit heroin more than doubled between 1969 and 1972—the latest figure reported—but are still fewer than five hundred a year. Those convicted for illegal possession of heroin or any other narcotic, or of one of the major hallucinogens, can be sent to jail for seven years—fourteen if they've been dealing in the drug or manufacturing it— and can be fined any amount the judge determines.

There is a shadow zone in the statistics of English addiction. As can be shown in several ways, some narcotics users are not attending clinics. How many? Because nobody is quite sure, Chinese heroin is worrisome. And yet the shadow zone existed before Chinese heroin appeared. As soon as the clinics were operating, a new statistic became possible—the clinics' muster of addicts actually under treatment, as totted up by the Department of Health. That figure leaped up to 1,171 by the end of June 1968, then advanced, much more slowly, to 1,241 on the last day of that year. But the Home Office index showed a total of 2,240 heroin addicts that year. Where were the missing 999? (When I asked Martin Mitcheson, he snapped, "Prison, hospital, or India.") The gap has been used by the Bureau of Narcotics and Dangerous Drugs, among others, as evidence that the British clinics are reaching "less than fifty per cent of the addict population." But part of the gap is clearly unreal. The Home Office index number, though it contained few duplicate entries, was cumulative through the year, and it included those who showed up once or twice at a clinic and got themselves notified to the Drugs Branch yet were not truly addicted and never returned. Just as clearly, part of the gap is real. And evidently it left room for a bureaucratic confrontation. At any rate, since 1969 the Home Office has offered two sets of index figures—not without internal grumbles. As always before, there are cumulative totals for the year. But now there are also totals for those known to be addicted on the last day of the year, and these figures are lower. Thus in the course of 1969 the index accumulated 2,881 addicts, of whom 2,480 were using heroin or methadone or both. But for the single day, 31 December 1969, the index showed only 1,466 addicts of all kinds, of whom 1,215 were using heroin or methadone or both—and this corresponded to the Department of Health's figure of 1,235 addicts under treatment.

A fringe exists, as every clinic director knows, if only because his addicts tell him they have friends who use narcotics but who are not enrolled at a clinic. These are the adolescents who wait two or three years between their first

HOW THE PROBLEM LOOKED IN 1970

	1968	1969		1970	
		cumula-tive total	Decem-ber 31	cumula-tive total	Decem-ber 31
All addicts of all narcotics (Home Office)	2,782	2,881	1,466	2,661	1,430
Heroin and metha-done addicts (Home Office)	2,240	2,480	1,215	2,233	1,175
Under treatment for addiction, all narcotics (Dept. of Health)	1,241		1,235		1,253

The Home Office grand total, across the top line, includes people addicted to morphine, pethidine, dextromoramide, and other morphine-related drugs or synthetics; most of these are addictions originating in medical treatment for something else.

shot of a narcotic and their first trip to a clinic or who try a clinic once and don't like it. But these are also the ones who experiment and don't get hooked. How one estimates the size and seriousness of the fringe determines how one judges the success of the clinics at containing addiction and bringing addicts into care; at issue, once again, is the definition of the addict and the possibility of the occasional user. But the fringe cannot in any case be large. Even a deliberately pessimistic calculation from the Addiction Research Unit in the spring of 1973 reckoned that there were no more than four hundred addicts not on the index.

The threat of the black market has grown real enough, though, to give a sharp polemical edge to the first fundamental disagreement about British drug-addiction policy that has arisen in England since the clinics themselves were decided on. The great surprise about the British clinics is how very little heroin they now in fact prescribe, and how deeply divided they have become about the drug. "When the American doctor visits the English clinics, he is appalled to find that they are all doing something different," Griffith Edwards said. "We have no White House drug coördinator in this country, no czar telling the clinics what to do." Given the professional independence of British medicine, it takes a conscious mental strain to visualize a politician or a civil servant directing treatment policies from, say, a "Special Action Office of No. 10 Downing Street." One thing that has never been changed is that the choice of treatment—heroin, methadone, or nothing at all—is the doctor's, not the patient's; and there are as many British systems of narcotics control, clinic staff maintain, as there are consultant psychiatrists running clinics. At All Saints' Hospital in Birmingham, John Owens' clinic still prefers to prescribe heroin except when the addict himself asks to change to methadone. At Glenside Hospital in Bristol, Ian Pierce James refuses to treat heroin addicts with any kind of injectable narcotic. At several provincial drug-treatment centers, the refusal to prescribe heroin for outpatients is so absolute that the Department of Health and even the local police have raised alarmed questions. Similar divergences of practice characterize the clinics in London. James Willis, who is in charge of the Drug Addiction Unit at St. Giles' Hospital there, has the reputation among other consultants and addicts for being relatively liberal with heroin. In a recent conversation, Dr. Willis said, "The thing is, doctors are influenced by an idea that's never been proved, namely that methadone is somehow 'better' than heroin." Willis is one of those who have raised the question whether a small gray market in British heroin tablets —that is, the addicts dealing among themselves in any excess from their prescriptions—many not be preferable to Chinese or French heroin. Addicts who report to the Drug Treatment Center of St. Mary's Hospital, which is in an area of some strategic importance—the Notting Hill district, where the last of the West End flower children have gone to seed—complain that it takes at least six weeks to be taken on, during which their only source of drugs is the black market. At many of the clinics, they complain that they are forced to change to methadone. And because transfers from one clinic to another are so rarely allowed, addicts say also that they have been deprived of any semblance of choice of drug or treatment— however great the variety of approaches the clinics may exhibit. The conflicts among the clinics are muted as yet. But the issues are the most fundamental of all: the use of heroin itself, and the proper role of the clinic in relation to the addict and to the community.

Methadone is one focus of the controversy. Some clinic directors say that the drug is the worst borrowing they could have made from the United States. But the two countries use methadone so very differently that American specialists often think their British colleagues have completely missed the point of the drug; British doctors, in turn, believe that the Americans, desperately searching for a "clean" alternative to the absolute evil of heroin, are concealing from themselves the dangers of methadone. The I. G. Farbenindustrie laboratory at Höchst am Main created methadone in the search for a morphine substitute late in the Second World War, when Germany was cut off from opium supplies. Yet it is a narcotic —an "opioid"—for its action is fundamentally similar to that of morphine or heroin, and it is as addictive. In American practice, methadone is always given by mouth, as a substitute for heroin by needle. It is normally taken in Tang or Kool-Aid, ersatz drug in plastic drink. Given by mouth, methadone has two qualities over which there is no dispute: it can prevent heroin-withdrawal symptoms while producing little or no euphoria, and it is long lasting, so that one dose can replace the heroin addict's five or six daily shots, with their time-devouring swings from restlessness to preparing the injection to euphoria to stupefaction. Dispute begins with the other qualities claimed for methadone. The original American technique, publicized by Vincent Dole and Marie Nyswander in New York City in the early 1960s, builds the addict up to large doses—a hundred milligrams or more a day. The claim was that the addict's nerves become so saturated with the narcotic that he could not enjoy heroin even if he did inject some. Dr. Dole and Dr. Nyswander called this "the methadone blockade." An alternative American procedure, developed by Jerome Jaffe at the end of the decade, when he was directing the addiction program of the state of Illinois, uses methadone in lower doses, in what amounts to a direct bid to undercut the illicit market—that is, as a cheap and legal way to maintain an addict. Followers of both Dole and Jaffe usually take it for granted that methadone should be a long-term, even a lifetime, addiction.

Methadone has its critics in the United States, who make a number of charges against it. That the methadone blockade is phony, a much overstated figure of speech, and that the addicts who volunteer for methadone programs are probably ready to stabilize their use of narcotics anyway. That withdrawal from methadone is more difficult and uncomfortable than withdrawal from heroin. That replacement of one addiction by another seems no great gain, since a serious black market in methadone has sprung up in New York and, particularly, in Washington, where, it is said, those addicted to methadone now outnumber heroin addicts (this market has so far been supplied with methadone diverted from legal sources, but illegal synthesis demands neither technical virtuosity nor imported ingredients). That at most American methadone clinics one of the greatest problems is alcoholism (although good pharmacological research is still lacking, many critics believe that methadone facilitates drunkenness, and possibly makes other drugs more attractive as well, to a degree that heroin does not). Such objections have especially aroused American blacks, whose leaders often speak as though they believed methadone maintenance had been plotted to sedate ghetto protest; on that semantic scale, proposals for heroin maintenance are attacked as "genocide." Within American city and federal bureaucracies, whose addiction programs are increasingly committed to methadone, criticism has been more scattered. But it is true, for example, that when Graham Finney, the director of New York City's Addiction Services Agency, quit that job at the end of 1972, he gave as one reason his mistrust of methadone and the good-guy image of it that has been so energetically promoted.

English clinics use methadone not only orally but also by injection. Doses by mouth are low. Doctors there have no faith in methadone blockade and see no point in putting an addict on the long-term high dosage that the blockade theory requires; they say it's too difficult to get his dosage down again. Methadone syrup is prescribed for the new addict at some clinics, and universally for the addict who requests it in the last weeks or days of progressive withdrawal from all narcotics. But the British practice that shocks American specialists is the use of injectable methadone for addicts. The injectable methadone is prescribed in sterile ampoules, ten milligrams of methadone hydrochloride in solution. Its use with heroin addicts became general at the time the clinics were established, and this happened at first, in some part, because doctors new to drugs believed that American experience had proved methadone better than heroin, but grossly misunderstood how Americans used it. Poignantly, English addicts have also absorbed the idea from the United States that methadone is better; though they almost always prefer the effects of heroin, they almost always feel that a switch to methadone represents a step toward cure. An addict may request the change, even when he is not prepared to give up the needle. Simply this aspect of methadone—the addicts' own belief that it symbolizes a readiness to try to live more stably—appears to explain the good reports some English clinics make about the drug. But even the testimonials can take strange twists. Thomas Bewley, who directs the drug-dependence clinic at Lambeth Hospital, said, "As far as my patients are concerned, the ones on heroin are all doing much better in their lives than those on methadone. But that result is a complete artifact, don't you see. Because whenever I have an addict who is doing badly, I switch him onto methadone. I think that even in the States, if you take your drugs fairly sensibly, you can hold down your life." Methadone taken intravenously loses many of its reputed advantages. It is as likely as heroin to cause the spread of diseases, like serum hepatitis, that come from passing around a dirty syringe. And, though oral methadone may produce no euphoria, when enough of the drug is injected it will certainly produce a high that most addicts say is nearly as delightful as heroin's. For that reason, and also because a drug when taken intravenously is excreted more quickly than when taken orally, addicts who take methadone by needle are likely to inject themselves frequently enough to lose much of the gain of a longer-acting drug.

Once the clinics were functioning smoothly, the doctors' inclination to switch addicts to methadone was reinforced by mutual example; as heroin doses became smaller, competition developed to demonstrate success by cutting heroin use still further. Under all these pressures, though the total number of people addicted to heroin or methadone or both has remained more or less steady, methadone has supplanted heroin as the drug most commonly used by addicts; in 1972, only 442 addicts known to the Home Office were taking heroin alone. Clinics report that they now get new patients who started by injecting methadone rather than heroin. The total amount of heroin prescribed in August 1968, the peak month at the clinics, was 3,209 grams—over seven pounds. By the summer of 1971, less than two-fifths that much heroin was being prescribed by the clinics, and consumption now seems to have stabilized at just under 1,200 grams a month. Methadone use has meanwhile climbed steadily: the latest figures available, for the summer of 1973, are also the highest so far, and show the clinics prescribing over 2,300 grams a month, two-thirds of that in injectable form, one-third by mouth. And though doctors outside clinics may legally prescribe methadone for addicts, not many do. Methadone has not been importantly misprescribed, as heroin was by general practitioners in the early 1960s; nor will it ever be, for in 1973 new regulations came into force— forty-seven years after the Rolleston Committee's report—that give the Home Office power to hale a doctor before an extraordinary professional tribunal, which can take away his right to prescribe particular substances, like methadone or amphetamines. Nonetheless, to compound the clinics' problems, a gray market in English methadone ampoules has sprung up, addicts trading their clinic supplies among themselves for other drugs or selling the surplus outright. Many people who are close to the problem believe that such dealing in methadone may be as serious a danger as Chinese heroin.

Meanwhile, at one clinic in London a study has begun which will, for the first time, compare the fates of addicts maintained on heroin with a matched group maintained on oral metha-

done. New heroin addicts showing up at this clinic, once verified, are assigned at random to get one drug or the other; their
progress or deterioration, medically and socially, is watched.
The study promises to be extremely important, and it will take
at least three years to complete, in part because so few new
addicts are appearing these days.

The addiction clinic of Charing Cross Hospital, in central
London, lives in a shop across the street from the back entrance
to the hospital proper. A plastic sign by the door identifies it
as the hospital's "psychiatric unit annexe." A smaller plate by
the doorbell advertises that antenatal classes are held there.
Within, the clinic is a puzzle box of partitions and tiny offices.
Gisela Brigitte Oppenheim, who has directed the clinic since it
opened, in February 1968, is a handsome, dark-haired, briskly
sensible psychiatrist, somewhat of the pull-yourself-together-
man persuasion. On the spectrum of English clinic opinion,
Dr. Oppenheim is known to be generally opposed to prescribing heroin. She has an excellent reputation for getting addicts
into jobs and off drugs. "We have seen between seven hundred
and eight hundred addicts, or more," Dr. Oppenheim told me.
"We have around ninety-five current attenders, and eighty-five
or ninety others who at this moment are off drugs altogether
and are being followed up in the community. If a new addict
walked in the door today, from ten days to a fortnight would
pass before he had a script. We always tell them, 'If you're in
severe withdrawal, come in,' but no patient has ever taken us
up on that. We insist on three positive urine tests, several days
apart. You certainly can't go by the state of their arms. Many
will come in here to try to get an injectable narcotic with the
idea of selling it to get soft drugs. When we *are* convinced,
we offer the new patient methadone syrup. If we can't get
away with that, injectable ampoules. I haven't prescribed

heroin for a new patient in three years. Most who come in are poly-drug abusers, and settle for methadone. On heroin, it is much more difficult for them to function in the community. Currently, we have only two patients left who are on heroin only. And they are *chaotic*: it's a full-time job for an addict to be on heroin; injections are necessary every four or six hours, and in their condition, they can take anywhere from twenty minutes to an hour just to get a fix organized. We have ten other patients who are getting some heroin in addition to their methadone.

"When we started, our brief from the Ministry of Health supposedly was, 'You maintain the addicts until they are motivated to go into hospital to get off drugs.' But when we started we had no inpatient facilities; we were obliged from the beginning to work in a way that would get the patients into condition to function in the community. In our experience, many addicts who are detoxified as inpatients go back on drugs when they get back into the community. If we had an inpatient unit now, we wouldn't know what to do with it. Sixty-five per cent of our current attenders are gainfully employed—some work as laborers, one is a teacher, several have gone back to their university courses. They can be so stable that nobody would guess they were addicts. Once they are working, once they have other interests, personal relationships, they get fed up with the drug life. It isn't a conscious decision; it just happens. In many cases, we can't explain just how and when this point is reached —certainly it's nonsense for the doctor to claim the credit. Our psychiatric approach is supportive and not analytical—perhaps, in American terms, nonpsychiatric. We have two full-time social workers. The addicts get a great deal of help with simple practical matters—accommodations, food. The important thing is to teach them that there is an alternative to the way they were living when they first came in. We want them to mix with non-addicts. It is very important to have their leisure time organized. We often find that the addict makes a complete break with the drug-taking group that he has been involved with before he is able to kick the drug habit."

A civil servant from New York City remarked to me that he came away from a four-day visit to the British clinics questioning whether they would be conceivable outside the total setting of the National Health Service, with its presumption of universal free medical care, its rational administration, and its controlled costs. The question is a sophisticated one—or, at least, it has different answers at different levels. "In policy discussions, I now ask, 'If we are interested in the British approach to drugs, are we willing to build the underpinning that seems to be the key?' " he said.

When the American visitor first asks what the British clinics cost, he gets the wonderful reply not that the figures aren't published but that they aren't even known. "Administratively, our 'drug program' doesn't really exist," an observer told me. "There's no coördinating point. And we don't separate the figures any more than the functions." But when I penetrated to the right bureaucrat, "costing the clinics" seized him as a refreshing and possibly useful American sort of idea; so after three months a letter arrived from the Department of Health and Social Security setting out "the respective annual costs of Clinic A and Clinic B" in terms that agreed well with the back-of-an-envelope reckonings of a couple of clinic directors. The numbers of addicts attending clinics A and B full time are certainly typical. The staffs quoted for them seem slightly below the levels at most clinics I have observed; personnel were figured in fractions of a five-and-a-half-day week, then priced at the top of each Health Service pay category at that time—£7,348 ($17,635) a year for the full time of a consultant psychiatrist, £5,313 ($12,751) for a physician as medical assistant, £1,800 ($4,320) for each nurse, and so on. The cost of dispensing heroin and methadone by pharmacists was excluded here, but given at the end of the letter. Including rent and utilities, the cost of Clinic A, which had ninety-five pa-

CLINIC A

Staff	£	
Consultant (4/11*)	2,672	
Medical Assistant (15/11*)	7,245	
Assistant Matron (full time)	2,073	
Sister (two, full time)	3,600	
Social Worker (full time)	1,932	
Secretary/Receptionist	1,311	
Total for staff	18,833	
Overheads (rent, rates, electricity, etc.—estimate)	2,415	
Total	£21,248	($53,120)
Number of patients: 95		

CLINIC B

Staff	£	
Consulant (2/11*)	1,336	
Medical Assistant (full time)	5,313	
Sister (full time)	1,800	
Social Worker (full time)	1,932	
Assistant Social Worker (full time)	1,395	
Total for staff	11,776	
Overheads (estimate)	2,500	
Total	£14,276	($35,690)
Number of patients: 75		

"This gives an annual cost for treating each patient of £224 for Clinic A and £190 for Clinic B. . . . The annual cost of drugs on the special forms used for prescribing to addicts is approximately £129 for each patient."

* Half-day sessions, based on 5½-day week.

tients, was £21,248 ($50,995) a year—£224 ($538) a patient.
For Clinic B, which had seventy-five patients, the cost was
£14,276 ($34,262)—£190 ($456) per patient. Separately figured, the annual cost for drugs prescribed to addicts was about
£129 ($310) for each patient. The overall total came to be-
tween $800 and $850 per English addict per year.

There the British calculation stopped. American pay scales
and rents would multiply these figures by three or more, bringing the cost to at least $2,400 a year per addict, as long as doc-
tors and nurses did not become scarce. Greater precision is not
really possible. Yet it is evident that because, after all, the number of addicts has never been really large or out of control,
the English have been able to put a disproportionately great
investment of money and of trained people into their care.

Hackney Hospital is ten miles northeast of Charing Cross.
It is set down among terrace rows of housing—not the cream
and white town houses that swell along the great leafy squares
of the West End, but narrow-shouldered mud-gray brick rows,
block after block. The Special Psychiatric Unit at Hackney
Hospital is directed by Dr. John L. Reed, but he turned me
over to the man who, he said, does the work—a psychiatrist
named John Mack. Dr. Mack, slight, dark-bearded, and looking
nearly as pale and young as some of his clients, has opinions
about heroin that are at the other end of the spectrum from
Dr. Oppenheim's. He had with him a buxom girl with massed,
brilliant red hair—Susan Norvill, one of his social workers.

"I'm very angry at you Americans," Mack began. "For getting us started with methadone." I pointed out that injectable
methadone is not used in the United States. "Unfortunately,
that didn't come across clearly in 1968," he said. "There *is* a
black market now, and it is flourishing—in Chinese heroin, as
the clinics stop prescribing heroin and go over to methadone.

And in methadone itself. What worries me is that some clinic people, thinking that methadone is somehow preferable, are giving fairly large prescriptions. And the methadone is being sold."

"We've seen primary methadone addicts who have never tried heroin," Miss Norvill said.

I mentioned methadone blockade. "I inherited two cases," Mack said. "By the way, what *do* you call addicts? They're not patients in the classical sense, *not* 'cases'—the best word, I think, is 'clients.' Two clients, then, who were both taking 225 milligrams of methadone a day by mouth—that's twice the blockade level—and also taking twenty milligrams of heroin a day by injection, and getting *great* pleasure out of it. The morality of giving methadone for a very long term by mouth—surely there's an element of self-delusion? I use methadone for only two reasons now. Some people come here addicted to methadone, and it doesn't quite make sense to insist that they switch to heroin. Or, because methadone has been presented to the world as the drug of therapy, the addict sometimes thinks he is progressing if he switches.

"Too many of us in England are still pursuing the medical model of treating addiction," Mack said. "But although we are doctors, in National Health Service clinics, the people who come to us are people using drugs—not people coming to a doctor asking for help and advice in the traditional relationship. I don't think that you can hope to solve a society's drug problem by pharmacology. You can't cure heroin addiction by giving methadone. The concept of the wicked drug with its claws in them—take that away and you would abolish the problem: this misses the point.

"When we started, in 1968, we could divide our clients into three groups," Mack said. "Most were working-class youths—

almost all boys, seventeen, eighteen, nineteen years old, living with their parents at home. They had jobs, and were in every way ordinary. Then, a smaller number, somewhat older, above average in intelligence, not working—floaters, hippies, broken homes. And the third group, the old-time prescription addicts, sometimes in their forties, who had been on heroin a very long time. One felt pretty hopeless about them. Since that time, the new ones who have been coming to us are almost all working class, and almost all adolescents, though recently they have been a little older."

What he said reminded me that I had been told elsewhere that the average age of the addicts showing up at the clinic doors since they were first opened had been rising by nearly one year every year. The rise has continued at least through 1972, the latest published figures. The figures also show— and it is one of the most encouraging signs of all—that even though the total number of addicts has held fairly constant, the percentage under twenty has dropped sharply. At the end of 1972, only three addicts as young as sixteen were known in Britain, and only thirteen aged seventeen. (These, by the way, are treated like any others at English clinics, while in America, with depressing illogic, addicts under eighteen are not supposed to be admitted to methadone programs—though, of course, some are.) Asked about the rise in age, Mack said, "Yes, recently the new clients have been about twenty-one. Often, they had their first try of heroin about the same time the others did—though their really full-scale *involvement* with heroin, or methadone, is likely to have started only three to six months before they come to us. But, as I say, they usually knew our regulars, hung around with them. Most of the people we get here were, in some way, influenced by that big explosion in the late '60s."

"The new thing is that they're marrying," Susan Norvill said. "A lot of ours now have young wives and babies. One would have hoped, naïvely, that forming a relationship with somebody would stabilize them. But many of them have *very* bad, messy marriages."

I asked how many new addicts they were getting. "Oh, maybe two a week," Mack said. "A lot of those are reappearing —after a stretch in prison, say. First, we'll ask where they live— with fourteen operating clinics around London, we all tend to throw people back to the clinic nearest to them. It's important to realize that people are not addicted as isolated individuals. They are addicted in relation to the community or the immediate small group. So if somebody really new comes to us, we have almost certainly heard of him from our regular clients months, even years, before—or, at least, it will turn out that we know his friends."

I mentioned the American stereotype of the English clinic bargaining with addicts over prescriptions. "God, that would be awful!" Mack said. "No. One doesn't spend a lot of time with them talking about drugs. The addict knows that it's expected that eventually he will come off. But that isn't our only aim. Really, attaining social stability, settling back into society, getting a job—I'd put all that ahead of getting off drugs." Then Mack added—and his statement demonstrates just how sharply clinic directors are divided—"I reject completely the notion, which came from America, that you can't work and be stable on heroin."

"Last time we counted, which was last spring," Miss Norvill said, "seventy-two per cent of our clients were working, and thirty per cent had regular, long-term jobs. And about that last figure, remember that a lot of our East London working-class youth change jobs often anyway."

"The clinic makes a therapeutic setting possible," Mack said. "Also, I'm protected by a certain amount of mutual observation, censoring by my colleagues. And I know they're there. Working with addicts is a pretty stressful thing. One has to be watched."

But is it really possible, just physically, to maintain addicts on heroin? Don't they deteriorate? Don't they get hepatitis, abscesses, damaged hearts and livers? "It can be hard to get them to use good injection techniques," Mack said. "But that's still looking at the wanderers only, the worst ones, the extremely unstable. Looking at our steady addicts, the ones who have been with us from the beginning, on heroin, I'd say very few are *worse*. And many are a lot less scruffy."

"As for the wanderers," Miss Norvill said, "without the clinics, they'd all be dead."

I asked about withdrawal. "We've honestly not seen anybody in severe withdrawal," they both said. "I think there is a physical withdrawal effect," Mack said, "magnified no end by mythology and drifting into an acute anxiety state." I brought up the recent reports that babies of addicted mothers show great distress within hours of birth. "Mothers and babies—the American literature is full of the problem," Mack said, with evident perplexity. "We have now had three addicted mothers have their babies, and, apart from putting the babies into a premature unit just so we could keep a close eye on them, we did nothing. And we observed no withdrawal signs. Not even increased restlessness.

"As far as I am aware," Mack said, "apart from the dangers that go with intravenous injections, there is no real evidence that the body cannot tolerate heroin for years. And you do not need to increase the dose, the way American doctors tell me. Given an unlimited supply, yes, most addicts—not all—

would tend to increase the dose. And if you do increase the dose you tend to spend all your life preparing the next injection and you do deteriorate. But if you have some supervision you don't deteriorate."

"We have very few who are in a socially deteriorated condition," Miss Norvill said.

"We have very many who are much more socially integrated than before," Mack said.

We talked about ways to promote social integration. At Hackney Hospital group therapy is sometimes used. Susan Norvill runs a group for wives who are not themselves addicts. "I thought that their husbands were getting a lot, actually, here, but that the wives were terribly isolated by the problems," she said.

Mack spoke of two groups among the addicts, one a group of eight that had been running for eighteen months. "Measured in terms of getting people off drugs, it has been fairly successful. But the ones who could never be reached for more than grunts," he said, "still grunt."

Mack paused, and then said, "I'm rather—irritated, by the North American system. Most of its virtues are based on doing the best you can without heroin. If we're not careful in this country, we are going to miss the big chance—because *here* we still have sufficiently few addicts so that we should be able to attend to *everybody*."

3

The Unfinished Business
of the Society

The idea that the United States should experiment with making heroin legally available to addicts has been advanced in several versions over the past decade. These suggestions—though, without fail, they cite the British experience of lawful heroin—have not come from the British specialists, but have been put forward by Americans. The British working in addiction are not ignorant of the American drug problem: just as American doctors and administrators have been visiting London by the score since the clinics opened, most of the leading British specialists have found a conference or a grant to bring them over to see what's being done about drugs in New York, Washington, perhaps elsewhere. The traffic in ideas about control of narcotics has been vigorous between the two countries. Nonetheless, the British have good reason to think that their approach to addiction is still oversimplified by Americans, not least by those who propose that government clinics to dispense heroin to addicts should be tried in the United States. English visitors who have spent time and thought on the American drug problem are troubled, of course, by many things they have seen. Certain observations recur. Even before the visitor has worked through his inevitable first impressions of size and complexity, he is likely to be struck by the sense of fear that pervades the American reaction to narcotics addiction, among professionals as well as ordinary people. The next time I saw Martin Mitcheson was not at his London clinic, but in Washington, at the offices of the Drug Abuse Council, in the spring of 1973, when he was near the end of a two-month tour that had taken him as far as San Francisco and New Orleans. "My impression is one of total confusion, really," Dr. Mitcheson said. "Because there are enormous and paradoxical differences in your drug scene between one city and another. And also because yours is a culture, after all, that is alien to me. And when I'm in England, I can think coherently about the steps in the whole addiction process, I can think about precipitating factors, I know my English addicts, I know my English sociological scene, I know the areas of social stress where drugs of various kinds are being used. And I can see what are reasonable strategies to adopt. Where a medical strategy, or perhaps an almost totally nonmedical strategy, is more or less appropriate. Here, people tell me about heroin in the ghettos, people tell me about violence in the streets—while they're driving me through the streets of Chicago, with our safety belts fastened, in a large car, after downing large dry martinis. I mean, anyone can make slightly satirical comments about it; but as a visitor, though I can see that people are frightened about addiction, I can't really feel whether they are right to be frightened. Or not." The second discovery that the English visitor comes to is the enormous amount of money in drugs in America—and what shocks him is not the money in the criminal distribution of drugs, which he has heard about, but the hundreds of millions being spent legally, by governmental and

private agencies, on narcotics control. The next time I saw
Margaret Tripp was also in Washington at the offices of the
Drug Abuse Council in the spring of 1973; she was one of a
group of eight (the rest Americans) whom the council had
awarded yearlong fellowships for study and travel in the
United States, and she was then six months into hers. "I've
never had such a beautiful office," Dr. Tripp said, stroking
the teak. "In the fellows' first meeting, we sat down out there
in the conference room, and very quickly somebody asked,
what are we doing here with these large salaries? And then,
to the credit of this organization, they laid on for our first
weeks some very good, top-line people to come and talk to
us. One guy in particular talked about the financial and government side, and exposed us to the fact that this year for the
first time, more than a billion dollars will go into drugs.
Which is a lot of money." She had recently attended the fifth
annual conference on methadone treatment, held that year in
Washington, which had been organized, she said, like a trade
convention, with the ground floor given over to commercial
exhibitors' booths. "You should have been there. The conference was attended by three thousand people." Her voice
got quieter. "All those people were getting salaries." She
stopped abruptly. Then she said, "One of the statistics we were
told was that, currently, for every American addict in any kind
of treatment, there are two staff receiving salary."

Such perceptions of the American response to narcotics
addiction are not unique to visitors; they reinforce observations that some Americans have been making recently—for
example, in the final report of the U.S. National Commission
on Marihuana and Drug Abuse, which was issued, as it happened, three days after my conversation with Margaret Tripp,
and which warned in terms as vigorous as hers of "the drug
abuse industrial complex." But the point is that, in this Ameri-

can context of anxiety and such massive reaction, proposals to make heroin legally available to addicts strike the British not as being wrong, necessarily, but as being different from their own approach not only in important practical details but in fundamental motive and principle. To begin with, the British have always thought that the Americans seem narrowly, obsessively preoccupied with the one chemical, heroin—whether for fifty years as the problem or, in the present debate, as its own solution. "I suffer so much, here, from people telling me what my 'system' is," Tripp told me. "I find that it's almost impossible to do the one thing here that I thought I would be able to do, which was to talk to Americans about where the differences in approach really are. Very early on, I began to discover that people here come up to me and *tell me* the difference: 'You give heroin.' And that is the beginning and the end of the conversation. Because to them this is such a terrible thing. And also such a simple and chemical thing. And therefore they do not have to find out whether this difference is a real one—like how much difference there really is between heroin and methadone, for instance—and they don't have to consider at all whether there might be other differences. Beyond heroin. And far more fundamental to success or failure in dealing with addicts."

The most conspicuous proposal to give American addicts heroin—and the one that seems to have set the terms of the current discussion—is the plan that the Vera Institute of Justice announced in New York City in the spring of 1972, after having circulated a more primitive version to city and federal officials a year earlier. The Vera Institute is a small, adventuresome research foundation that has earned respect for certain of its enterprises in criminology, notably a study of prisoners' eligibility for bail which led to reforms that have kept many people out of prison while waiting for trial. The Vera Institute's fascination with the British approach to addiction has been long-enduring and ambivalent. In 1966, a year after the second report of the Brain Committee, when the English were well aware that they had an epidemic, a group from the Vera Institute visited London and came up with a grandiose scheme for joint Anglo-American research into the causes of heroin addiction, in England. The preface to the proposal said that the British had failed, and predicted, flatly, "By 1972 England will have 10,000 heroin users"—or, in an exact calculation, 10,819. The projected research came to nothing. The projected 10,819 addicts, seized upon by journalists and the Bureau of Narcotics, served several years' hard labor building up the American belief that the "British system" was a demonstrated flop; they figured in the thinking of the Home Office, too. By 1972, the Vera Institute's judgment, confuted, was reversed. The plan for an experiment with lawful heroin in New York credited the British "clinic system," as the single cause, with stabilizing the number of British addicts at a level below that of 1968—and enlisted the clinics' example, and borrowed some of their practices, in support of a treatment program whose stated aims were different. The Vera Institute made its plan public at a time when gloom was spreading widely in the United States over the results obtained by established modes of treatment, and radical alternatives were being urged. Abstinent therapeutic communities had helped some addicts to reconstruct their personalities; but when funding agencies began to demand that the communities' enthusiastic reports be evaluated more carefully, it turned out that the long-term rates of success, in fact, were low. Even if they had been higher, the communities' intensive methods made them inherently slow to multiply. Methadone-maintenance programs had grown very fast indeed, and by that spring had taken on somewhere between fifty and sixty-five thousand addicts across the country; but by then, also, it was becoming clear that many of their clients had turned to alcohol and other drugs, that unknown and possibly large amounts of methadone were leaking from some of the programs into the black market, and that a great many addicts were not ready to enroll themselves. Nelson Rockefeller, in a speech, tried out the idea that New York should intensify the enforcement approach: "Pushers to Get Life," said the headlines. The Bureau of Narcotics and Dangerous Drugs was completing a study that showed that the cheapest way to deal with addicts is by compulsory hospitalization; this caricature of the medical model was made still more grotesque by those—including some doctors and some black leaders—who talked about heroin addiction as though it really were an infectious epidemic disease, and should thus be treated by sequestering addicts in quarantine ("Put them on an island," one official said), for years if necessary. And at the other extreme, that spring, several political figures had begun saying that the only way to break the American connection between crime and heroin is to allow addicts to be maintained on the drug. This notion became fashionable. *The New York Times* disclosed that the Mayor's Narcotics Control Council had considered with interest the first draft of the Vera Institute's plan. In Washington, the Committee on Crime Prevention and Control of the American Bar Association recommended that test programs of heroin maintenance be started. An impulsive legislator introduced a bill in the New York State Assembly which would have opened heroin dispensaries for addicts. One serious advocate of the use of legal heroin alongside methadone maintenance and the various abstinent programs was Howard Samuels, chairman of New York's Off-Track Betting Corporation, warming up for his run for governor two years later. "We've already got heroin maintenance—on the streets of

New York," Samuels said. He had been closely associated with the Vera Institute in other projects; he was on the platform at the press conference when the new plan was announced. The timing and sponsorship of the plan certainly gave plausibility to the argument of its opponents that it was intended to be the first step toward full-scale heroin maintenance for American addicts.

The plan itself, though, drew back from any suggestion of maintaining addicts on heroin for a long or indefinite time. The Vera Institute asked to be allowed to test a different idea: that there are a lot of addicts who have not been willing to accept methadone maintenance, or submit to the discipline of an abstinent, therapeutic group, who could be attracted to a treatment clinic by the offer of free legal heroin for a relatively short period—a year at most—during which they could be stabilized, brought into a durable, therapeutic relationship with clinic staff, and transferred before the end of the year to one of the more conventional modes of treatment. The aim was to reach the addict who has not been reached by the other modes. The method would use heroin as "bait" to induce him to come to the clinic, where he would find every sort of help towards rehabilitation, from psychiatric counseling to a protected and unstressful job. This would not be heroin maintenance in the British sense at all, the Vera Institute said. But also, "By initially attempting to stabilize the patient on heroin —his drug of choice—the first treatment efforts can focus on issues other than forcing the patient to substitute the 'clinic's drug' for the 'patient's drug'." There is a sly, essential perversion in that "drug of choice," which is properly a medical-textbook phrase to designate the best of several drugs for a particular condition, to be chosen by the *doctor*—as, indeed, the drug prescribed for an English addict is chosen. That aside, the Vera Institute's argument is just the one advanced

by psychiatrists at British clinics, like Martin Mitcheson or
John Mack, who use heroin to work toward heroin detoxification. Yet the Vera Institute was ingenious in foreseeing political objections, ingenious even in technical details. Heroin
would be injected only at the clinic; the addict would visit the
clinic three, four, or five times a day, or would simply spend
most of his time there; the clinic would be set up in a non-
residential part of Manhattan. Bargaining between addict and
clinic over the dose would be met by inarguably rigid rules.
Whether the addict was also using black-market drugs would
be checked by frequent, randomly timed urinalyses; since the
clinic's heroin would be pure, the urinalyses, besides tests for
the usual substances, would look for the quinine with which
street heroin in New York City is heavily cut. In the first year
of the Vera Institute's experiment, a pilot group of thirty men
would be chosen, each of whom had been an addict for at
least three years, as proved by medical, police, or social-
agency records, and each of whom had been in a methadone-
maintenance program for at least two months, well before the
heroin experiment was announced, but had failed, either by
dropping out or being thrown out. If even fifteen of the pilot
thirty stayed with the clinic, stabilized their dosages, and by
year's end were successfully transferred to oral methadone or
taken off drugs altogether, then a second, larger test of the
scheme would begin. This would compare the fates of another
hundred addicts at the heroin clinic with a matched group
of equal size given the complete psychiatric and social services
but maintained on oral methadone. The entire experiment
would last four years and cost about a million dollars.

As it turned out, the differences in purpose, technique, and
political finesse that were claimed for the Vera Institute's proposal mattered much less, for its reception, than the fact that
this was the first plan to try legal heroin for American addicts

which seemed fully worked out and which seriously asked for
a decision. Opinion polarized along the simplest lines. Passionate opposition to the proposal built up even before it was
publicly announced. It brought together black leaders, conservative politicians, the Bureau of Narcotics and Dangerous
Drugs, *The New York Times,* partisans of abstinent therapeutic
communities, and pioneers of methadone maintenance, in a
rare unity. They protested the danger of making any exception
to the American prohibition of heroin—and, almost without
fail, cited the British experience as evidence. Congressman
Charles Rangel, whose district includes Harlem, told the
House of Representatives that "it is imperative that we dispel
some of the myths about the British system of drug treatment
so that the American people will open up their eyes and
recognize heroin for what it is—a killer, not a drug on which
a human being should be maintained. . . . The truth is that
the failure of the English to control addiction since the beginning of the 1960s has them fumbling for a solution just as we
are." John Ingersoll, then director of the Bureau of Narcotics
and Dangerous Drugs, tuned his rhetoric to his audience when
he told a convention of California police chiefs, in May, that
"we are once again hearing of proposals for the establishment
of heroin maintenance clinics. We had first-hand opportunity
to review a so-called research proposal of this kind and quickly
discovered that it had virtually no support within the knowl-
edgeable scientific community and that most of those advocat-
ing this approach had already made up their minds as to the
conclusions which will be derived. They persist in subscribing
to an idealized view of the so-called British system which the
British authorities themselves would not support. These programs would provide intravenous injections of heroin including a lounge or 'nodding room' reminiscent of the opium dens
of a by-gone century. . . . Free heroin is not going to solve

the crime problem in the United States just as it has not solved the crime problem in Great Britain. What is going to contribute to its solution is the elimination of heroin addiction. What is the price we would have to pay for legalizing heroin in this fashion? First, it would be a virtual announcement of medical surrender on the treatment of addiction and would amount to consigning hundreds of thousands of our citizens to the slavery of heroin forever." Congressman Peter Peyser of upstate New York introduced bills in the House of Representatives specifically to outlaw use of heroin "in any drug maintenance program"; he got President Nixon's endorsement. Vincent Dole, the specialist in metabolic diseases who had invented the "methadone blockade" theory and had opened the first methadone-maintenance clinic in the United States, put the weight of his reputation into a signed editorial in *The Journal of the American Medical Association,* June 12:

Proponents of the heroin clinics appear to believe that 250,000 addicts could be kept happy with a daily ration of this drug, and thereafter would desist from crime. No one familiar with the pharmacology of heroin could make such an assumption. Heroin addicts cannot be maintained with a stable dosage. . . . Undoubtedly it would be possible to operate a small demonstration program (25 to 50 patients) if a large and experienced staff were available to negotiate with the patients on dosage and supervise their outside activities, but this would hardly be a realistic model for treatment of 250,000 heroin users. . . . What is most puzzling n the argument for heroin clinics is the claim that the dispensing of heroin is needed to bring addicts into methadone programs.

Judianne Densen-Gerber, a psychiatrist and lawyer who directs Odyssey House, an abstinent, therapeutic program in New York (she titled her autobiography *We Mainline Dreams*), said that "heroin maintenance is at least an honest admission that you can't do anything. Heroin is giving up.

Methadone is a lie." James Markham, an able journalist who
writes about drugs for *The New York Times,* reviewed the
controversy ignited by the Vera Institute, concluded the proposal was a bad idea, and interviewed a Swedish psychiatrist,
Nils Bejerot, who has studied the epidemiology of drug crazes
in several countries; if the United States adopted the "British
system," Dr. Bejerot told Markham, "you could easily get up
to three or four million addicts in five years. . . . Heroin
maintenance? Only those who don't know anything about addiction can discuss it."

That June, the Bureau of Narcotics and Dangerous Drugs
published what amounted to its counter to the Vera Institute's
proposal: a cost-benefit analysis, written under contract by
William McGlothlin and three colleagues in the Department of
Psychology at the University of California, Los Angeles, in
which they tried to compare various approaches to treating
addiction by computing, for each one, what they called the
"social profit"—meaning the direct and indirect savings to the
national economy that would result from adopting the method
of treatment, after subtracting nationwide running costs. The
McGlothlin report was a coarse-gained example of the cost-
benefit genre. It set up seven "treatment modalities" in terms
of four sorts of "pre- and post-treatment social costs per addict
per year." The methods of treatment included heroin maintenance, conceived as "a program similar to that currently
existing in England," a couple of versions of methadone
maintenance, therapeutic communities—and civil commitment.
That last is a legal euphemism. The report defined civil
commitment as "a period of incarceration or compulsory
hospitalization followed by a period of parole or outpatient
supervision"; in California, the state where civil commitment
of addicts has been used most heavily, those two periods total
seven years, and in New York the total is three to four years.

The report noted that the courts in those states have been slow to commit addicts, apparently because "the rehabilitative aspects of the program have not demonstrated an effective cure for addiction, and . . . the alternative jail terms for most of the offenses are only a few months."

The four sorts of costs—that is, the direct and indirect savings—by which the methods of treatment were compared, are estimates of the value of addicts' thefts, of spending on measures against addicts' crimes, of "unemployment (foregone production)," and of treatment measures. The calculations, though, were double-jointed. The total value of thefts by American addicts—but this total was the outcome of a spectacular martingale: 375,000 addicts, the average addict spending 60 per cent of his time at liberty and not abstinent, needing a median twenty dollars a day for his habit, getting the required income 60 per cent from theft, of which 20 per cent is theft of cash and the other 80 per cent theft of goods for which the fence pays him 30 per cent of true value—was placed at $2.827 billion a year. The figure contrasted with some others. Governor Rockefeller, sending his new tough enforcement plan to the New York State legislature, estimated that addicts in his state alone stole $6.5 billion a year to pay for drugs. The Federal Bureau of Investigation, in its yearly Uniform Crime Reports, put the total national value of *all* thefts, burglaries, and robberies at $1.3 billion in 1970, $1.5 billion in 1971, $1.2 billion in 1972. McGlothlin's assertions about addicts' crimes were not consistent with other research by the Bureau of Narcotics and Dangerous Drugs: Ingersoll, in his speech that spring to the California police chiefs, warned that the relation of heroin to crime "has been greatly overstated," and said that one study by the bureau had just found that heroin addicts commit less than a quarter of all thefts by all kinds of drug users. The issue is crucial. In the McGlothlin report, addict thefts accounted for nearly two-thirds of the total amount that opiate addiction was said to cost the American economy. The *savings* in theft which the authors imagined would follow adoption of each of the seven hypothetical methods of treatment were an even larger—and highly variable—proportion of the seven "social profits'" they computed.

"The only significant information on heroin maintenance is provided by the British approach," the report said, and "the current British system is functioning reasonably well." But the authors misread their sources. They made the tired mistake of thinking that the English addict is free to choose heroin, injectable methadone, or oral methadone; they were thus talking, not about a medical, but about a drug-dispensary model of treatment, and so were understandably pessimistic about the chances that any great proportion of addicts would stabilize their lives. They also abused the British statistics. For example, they understated the Department of Health's year-*end* figure for addicts in treatment in 1970, loosely exaggerated the Home Office's index figure for the year-*long* cumulative total of addicts of all narcotics (see table, page 106), and then mated these two creations to generate the statistical monster that "less than 50% of the addict population" has been attracted to the British clinics—which, if true, would score heavily against any proposed American experiment with heroin for addicts, and especially against the Vera Institute's, for which the attractiveness of heroin is essential. Again, the report put a price on a heroin maintenance program "similar to that currently existing in England" of $1,500 a year per addict, for the first 50,000 addicts, and $1,000 each for the next 100,000, though the real British costs (see page 117) translated into American pay scales worked out in 1972 to at least $2,400 a year per addict, and economies of scale are not in sight. Such errors were the result of carelessness and incomplete information. But when the authors ignored the reflexive effects that implementing a mode of treatment for large numbers of addicts would have on the supply and cost of essential ingredients, like medical staff, then they abandoned the greatest justification of the cost-benefit method.

Assumptions about the amounts that addicts steal affect particularly the comparison that the McGlothlin report made between heroin maintenance and civil commitment, the two extremes of the seven treatment approaches. It costs a lot to keep addicts locked up, and not a little to keep them on tight parole, but the prevention of thievery can be presumed to be nearly total. In contrast, although the British police say that crime by addicts is not a problem, and credit the fact explicitly to narcotic maintenance through the clinics, McGlothlin and his colleagues supposed that reduction in theft in their hypothetical heroin program would be no better than fifty to seventy per cent. "Foregone production" was the next cost the authors listed, and it was far below addicts' thefts; the calculations were made by a mighty formula that spread across two pages, but when they figured the lost production that heroin maintenance would recover, they began with the assumption that these addicts are less employable than those maintained on methadone—a chief point, of course, that any experiment with heroin maintenance would be designed to test. The authors' reckonings were exclusively monetary; their sense of individual welfare or of civil liberties seems slight. They observed, in passing, that the first goal of the British approach is "to treat the addict in a non-compulsory manner." They explained that "the existing civil commitment programs have failed to accomplish their goal of controlling addiction because society is reluctant to deprive the addict of his freedom for such prolonged periods." But social terms had no place in their calculus of social profit. The report concluded that, with a sufficiently energetic program, "it appears probable that the large majority of the addict population would be committed within two or three years"; and if some therapeutic communities and a bucket of methadone were thrown in, the program would produce a net gain of at least $2.289 billion a year. Civil commitment all by itself would save $1.934 billion or more. Heroin maintenance might gain $1.573 billion a year—less than methadone maintenance. The conclusion is no surprise. Civil commitment is an approach to addiction the Bureau of Narcotics has favored for years. The influence of the McGlothlin report should not be overstated. Though it has circulated widely in Washington, it has not received the public scrutiny given to the Vera Institute's proposed test of a heroin clinic. It is significant, however, because the policy it frames is the radical alternative on the enforcement side.

When the excitement calmed, the effect of the Vera Institute's proposal was to force discussion—the first thorough, engaged, and consequential discussion—of the arguments for and against heroin maintenance in the United States. As one might expect, British observers are startled by the facility with which their experience is adapted to support almost any position in the American controversy. They themselves are scrupulous not to suggest that they have definitive lessons to teach, least of all about the broadest issues. The Vera Institute's particular variant of a heroin clinic, though, prompts several questions. "Why try such an experiment in New York City?" Martin Mitcheson asked. "I'm not sure you couldn't find thirty or 130 addicts in New York City who would show remarkable improvement in their lives by coming into a clinic to walk through hoops four times a day." In the late '60s, when the English were moving to set up their clinics and to restrict prescribing of heroin for addicts—a slight change compared to legalizing heroin in the

United States—the first outpatient drug-treatment clinic was the one begun by John Owens in Birmingham, where the number of addicts was relatively small and where the clinic had an immediate, important, measurable effect. Several English and American critics have suggested that any experiment like the Vera Institute's, to get clear and useful results, ought to be carried out in a town like, say, Portland, Maine, that is not one of the major centers of addiction. The Vera Institute's plan also envisions medically supervised injections at the clinic. Other American proposals for heroin maintenance have made the same provision. One can see the political, the public-health, and the police reasons: pure heroin is worth its weight in gold. Yet many American doctors are disgusted by the idea of supervising or administering narcotic injections to addicts; and the addict coming to the clinic for every shot, perhaps every five or six hours, would keep the clinic open around the clock, around the week. The British have never thought this would be practical, or attractive to addicts. Yet observers fear, perhaps rightly, that the British prescribing method would be too easily abused in the American setting. The dilemma is not easy to resolve. An assumption shared unthinkingly by all American comments on heroin maintenance is that addicts under twenty-one, or eighteen, would not be admitted. But heroin addiction in the present day is a problem of adolescence; more than half of American addicts have become addicted before they were twenty-one. English clinic directors do accept teen-age clients, with the usual precautions to make sure they are genuinely addicted. From London, the American prudishness about age seems grotesque. On the other hand, the Vera Institute's proposal counts on the use of intravenous methadone with some addicts at some times, as well as heroin; other American discussions of heroin maintenance, from the McGlothlin report to the Consumers Union study, also include injectable methadone as though its acceptability were a matter of course, once heroin is admitted. But British clinic directors, having begun the use of injectable methadone in part out of a misunderstanding of American methadone maintenance, urge that this is one of their clinic practices that Americans would be wise to examine skeptically. The Vera Institute's proposal raises more general questions, too. What would follow if the experimental clinic were judged a success? Suppose most of the thirty and then of the hundred addicts were stabilized on heroin and eventually graduated to oral methadone or to an abstinent community. Could the success—could the elaborate psychiatric and social services—of the experiment be duplicated on a large scale? Would the year's time limit for injectable opiates be retained? An experiment can't be conducted in isolation from the larger problems.

Opponents of heroin maintenance for the United States have a cluster of objections—often put with great emotional intensity—against the characteristics of the drug itself: that addicts given the choice will always prefer heroin, that it is not possible to stabilize heroin dosages, that heroin addicts lead chaotic lives. To these assertions, the English experience I think makes a clear response: heroin addicts differ; there can be stable heroin addicts, able to manage their doses and their lives, though these may not be the most usual and certainly are not the most noticeable; a clinic that offers sensible psychiatric and social services besides drugs, and where the physician can select other drugs besides heroin, can help a high proportion of its clients to live more healthily, more sanely, more effectively in society. The opponents' greatest fear is that heroin maintenance clinics in the United States would make addiction spread faster, lessening, implicitly, the social disapproval of heroin, decreasing the risks of experiment or occasional use —and even increasing the supply, since only the most wildly liberal clinics, they reason, could keep the addict from going right back to his illicit source for more. The danger of creating more addicts convinced the U.S. National Commission on Marihuana and Drug Abuse: "This speculation . . . we do believe . . . weighs heavily and tips the balance against heroin maintenance in this country at this time," the commission said in its final report. (It recommended, however, that "the federal government should sponsor a continuous and systematic examination of the heroin maintenance program in Great Britain, not only to find out how well it has worked there, but also to determine in what way the British experience would apply to the American situation, and what ways it would not.") Advocates of the use of lawful heroin for treatment of addicts say, on the contrary, that it would cut deeply into the criminal supply system, as well as reducing crime by addicts in pursuit of drugs. The Consumers Union report on drugs argued, for example, that heroin maintenance must be tested because "it is economically disastrous and morally indefensible to permit the American system of heroin distribution to flourish and to enrich itself—without even trying to find an alternative." These issues are peculiarly American, however. The British, grateful for the warnings they have taken from the United States, over many years, against tying addiction to crime, have nothing here to reëxport. England has never had an illicit system of drug distribution like the American one —large, rich, well-organized, and entrenched—with which the lawful prescribing of narcotics to addicts had to compete. American proponents say also that addicts would be better off, physically and socially, at a clinic, with pure cheap drugs and sterile syringes, getting at least a minimum of medical attention and of regular contact with clinic staff, than they are on the street; to keep addicts living as many of them do is intolerable. No English observer could disagree: the British experience is the embodiment, the dramatization, on a small scale, of what this argument means. Yet that by itself, however inspiring, is not particularly helpful, for it's also clear that there is no way the United States can simply duplicate the British approach; the real question is whether an American heroin program could be designed that does not carry unacceptable penalties.

"My feeling about heroin maintenance is that we have to try anything," I was told in England by an American who was there to work for some weeks at one of the drug clinics. He is Norman Zinberg, a psychoanalyst at Harvard, who in repeated visits has spent more than a year in England observing the British approach to addiction; he also had a hand in drafting the Vera Institute's proposal. We talked first while watching the peacocks on the lawn of an English country house where he was staying; we met again more recently at his house in Cambridge, Massachusetts. Dr. Zinberg is a man who sometimes says subtle things in a deceptively categorical manner. He holds that Americans, from the medical profession and the adolescents in contact with drugs to the general public, must transform their relationship to drugs, particularly heroin. He sees experiments with heroin maintenance as part of the process of taking the curse off the drug; but what he has learned from the English is not that their approach to heroin would work in the United States, but that it is possible to cultivate different social attitudes toward powerful drugs, attitudes which doubtless need to be taken further than the British themselves have yet succeeded in doing, but which, if they can be developed, may provide the only civilized hope of bringing the drugs under control. "With the number of people in pain in our ghettos, maybe there is a need for *something* legal," Dr. Zinberg said. "I feel that what we have to do is to develop reasonable social rituals governing the way we use drugs." Zinberg suggested comparison to alcohol and LSD. "Alcohol users, a hundred and fifty years ago or even less, were exactly the same as heroin users today. You were an addict, or you were abstinent—not even abstemious, you were abstinent. As many as eighty per cent of alcohol users were drunks, alcoholics. But alcohol now is very much socially ritualized, and in that context I think we have achieved a fair degree of control. Though *of course* I'm aware that it can be disastrous, and that it is a major problem for anywhere from five to eight million people in this country. But we have 120 million drinkers. And I can argue this in a lot of ways: I think that one of the ways we got control of caffeine was with coffee breaks and things like that—while one of the ways we didn't get control over nicotine is that we never could hold to the social rituals, no smoking until after dinner when the ladies had left the table, things like that. Some of which some people are now trying to reëstablish." He offered me a whisky, which I accepted. "Now when it comes to heroin, and the development of sustaining, informal controls: what the United States has done is to push these people, the addicts, outside of any such social control, while what the English have done—or, at least, begun to do within the framework of the clinics—is to establish viable social rituals for narcotics." Such controls are clearly the extension of the sorts of interactions within the small group by which initiation into drug use— whether smoking, drink, or the needle—takes place. Sometimes controls emerge, Zinberg said, even when the larger society has not tried to shape them. "With LSD, not just LSD but that whole group of drugs, I think we have had a paradoxical de- velopment. There's every indication that the use of these drugs is going up. But the pattern of use has changed. In the middle '60s, people who had discovered LSD were taking it two hun- dred, three hundred times, taking incredible quantities. And maybe a quarter of the people who were being admitted to Bellevue and Massachusetts Mental Health Center were on bad LSD trips. But today what you find instead is that people use LSD or mescaline or whatever three or four times a year; a small group of friends will go off, to a good place at a good time, and they're doing this very special thing—and they'll have what they regard as a pleasure, their expectations are reduced and reasonable, they're not pursuing a profound mystical insight and all that. And what they've done really is to establish social rituals and relate them to their own 'counter-cultural' institutional structures, and—gee! There hasn't been a bad trip in an American hospital for years, virtually. That's all gone. But use is up."

To find out more about social controls and heroin, Zinberg said, he has begun a study of occasional heroin users. "Increasingly I find in the United States—and I have a certain amount of research money to study this—that contrary to the conventional wisdom, which is that people who use heroin have to get addicted eventually, it seems to me it's quite possible to chip on heroin. What I've seen in England certainly suggests that. In our new study we're finding that chippers show very different patterns. There's the regular Saturday-night user. There are people who use for a while and then don't use for a while. There are spree users who then don't do it again for a long time. There are even *addicts* who cut down to chipping. We have a whole variety of chippers that we've found, not in enormous numbers yet, but with a lot of indication that many more are there. There's been very little in the literature about this so far." He mentioned the one study I had seen, Douglas Powell's preliminary report on twelve occasional heroin users, published in April 1973. "My hypothesis is that what keeps people from becoming junkies is just this matter of the extent to which the use is socially ritualized. One wants to be cautious in drawing conclusions. But the evidence seems to be that even heroin, and it's a very powerful drug, can really, under the right circumstances, be brought under the control of certain rituals. I'm certainly not suggesting it should ever be used as freely as alcohol; I'm just saying that these controls are not impossible even for so powerful a drug. People get a lot of control over highs—marijuana, LSD, even some junkies over heroin highs. What I've found so attractive in the English approach—and what I felt was extremely important for us to work towards, and to try to make some use of—is that through the clinics they are trying to get the addict into a relationship with a social institution in a way that is directly relevant to his drug use, and once he's there, to use the formalized and very sustaining social rituals of the doctor-patient relationship, the weekly visit and discussion, and the subsidiary informal relationships with the rest of the clinic, as a way to subject the heroin use to viable, accepted controls. The strength of the English approach to heroin is that they've tried this, and to some extent succeeded. And I argue very strongly that it is not a matter of cultural differences between us and the English; you can't just put it down to national character. Because look how badly the British have done with marijuana, you know? They've treated marijuana just as we did, as a police problem, a lot of people arrested, a lot of people sent to jail, it's become politicized—and they have developed the same kind of marijuana problem we have, growing use, growing anger in the colleges, political opposition, and the whole familiar thing. In the United States, with methadone, we are not really doing the same sort of thing the English have done with heroin. I think methadone is not as satisfactory as heroin: it's partly the drug perhaps, but more important, it's the addict's drug versus the clinic's drug. And methadone's by mouth, and a lot of people are hooked on needles. And except for Vince Dole's methadone clinic, where they tell the addict 'It's medicine, it's good for you,' everybody else in the United

States is hung up on the morality of the drug, and of drug use. Methadone is a bad thing, and 'yes, we're giving you this bad thing 'cause you do a worse thing otherwise, and as soon as we can we'll straighten you out and get you back on the right path.'

"We've shown, it seems to me, very little imagination, given the problem we have," Zinberg said. "Certain new things like heroin maintenance we've been unwilling to play with at all. The first thing we need is a number of experimental programs using heroin. The Vera Institute of Justice program is no great shakes as far as research or anything else goes, but it's a start. And we can design others, quite different heroin-maintenance programs, each experimental, each with only a small number of addicts. To break through all these questions —is it culturally different, can you compete with the pusher on the street corner, will the addict stabilize his dose?—all those things that have paralyzed us politically about getting heroin under control. We've got to move in and try things, even to find out that they don't work. We're so frightened of moving."

Back in London, I had lunch again with Griffith Edwards— a pizza and a Guinness at a pub near the Maudsley Hospital— and asked him what further an American might learn from the British experience with heroin addiction. "I still see the English clinic approach, for better or worse, as medical," Dr. Edwards said. "I don't see the American methadone clinics as medical, but as technological. In the American mind there seem to be these two strands—first, the fundamentalism, or salvationism, or utopianism, and second, the technological. I think the bitter enmity between your abstinent therapeutic communities and your methadone clinics embodies the deep schism in the American soul between its fundamentalism and its technology. Bear in mind that it may be totally naïve to expect that decisions in an area like drugs can be based on objective data or rational calculation.

"More than that—I want to warn you: to try to answer the question 'Should heroin be prescribed?' would be a dangerous narrowing down from the data you've got. The real questions to be considered have more to do with such things as the processes of decision making. And the relation of society to the individual. And the magnitude of a society's anxiety—anxiety to which drugs are a response, anxiety as a response to drugs, anxiety that creates the social distances from which society perceives those who take drugs. And eventually, yes, one must also reach this whole question of the ways that the individual is created and focused and controlled by the social forces that immediately surround him. Thus, heroin cuts to the unfinished business of the society. And of the understanding of society."

"There's nobody I love in America quite like your ex-addict," Margaret Tripp said, in Washington in 1973. "One of the things I ask people here—I know a guy, a beautiful guy, been on the street here for a long time, and survived, very active, intelligent, knows entirely where he is at: so I say to straight Americans, why do you have to turn this guy into somebody you label as a sick, inadequate personality who can't cope with life, in order for you to reëmbrace him, reintegrate him into society? Why do you not take him back on his own terms?" I asked her what answers she got. "No answers at all. I haven't had an answer yet. *My* answer is, of course, because he's a hustler. He's a good hustler. He is an image of the society. And you don't like that. And not only is this guy hustling, but he has preserved his freedom, the one thing the organization or corporate hustler knows he's given up. And the other thing, of course, that I notice: the first question an American is likely to

ask me is, 'What do you do about the pleasure? If you give
addicts heroin, do you give it to keep them straight or do you
give it for pleasure?' The heroin addict over here, it seems to
me, is perceived not only as a hustler, and one who is free,
but a guy who has access to pleasure. On a scale beyond the
imagination. Even though of course it is totally not true."

(Ideas reverberate. A year earlier, I had had a conversation
in New York with Graham Finney, then commissioner of the
city's Addiction Services Agency. Finney had recently returned
from a trip to England to visit the clinics; I was about to go.
One thing he said was, "I think, more and more, that the addict
is a caricature of American society—the hedonism, the demand
for instant gratification, the urge to get it now. He's a caricature
of many, many businessmen I've known." Later, he added,
"You know, in a funny way the addiction problem brings into
focus a lot of the unsolved business of this country.")

"I can't get American doctors, working in drugs, to see
themselves as part of the total scene," Tripp said. "In London, as we cut down on prescribing heroin, we'd hear about
it, we'd be told, 'The guys are taking methadone instead and
they're taking other things, amphetamines, barbiturates. You're
responsible.' So at the time, when you're in the middle of it,
you say no, I'm not responsible. And then you go away and
you think about it. And you know that it's there. That you
are part of the system that has moved the problem along.
American doctors just don't perceive themselves as factors
that cause change. When I was first here, I did a heavy stint
of going around Washington, talking to people who were
actually working on the streets, and to the guys themselves.
And this has been a real credit to the police and the B.N.D.D.—
the drug at the street level had been cut to the point where
it was less than two per cent heroin. The guys were injecting
quinine and hardly any heroin at all. Right then while the

people at the top level here were still talking about the heroin problem and what could be done about it, those who were on the streets of Washington, whether staff or patients, knew that nobody could *get* any heroin. So I said, 'What's the problem, then, mate?' And they said, 'Well we've got this terrible amphetamine problem, what is the solution?' And nobody saw the slightest connection between the one and the other. And in New York, as you probably know, the guys who are on methadone, if they want a party, they take wine, or alcohol—or cocaine. Cocaine is back on the streets in a big way. And it's an expensive drug."

(At the Anglo-American Conference on Drug Abuse, in London that spring, I met, for the first time, Daniel Freedman, Chairman of the Department of Psychiatry at the University of Chicago, who, I learned, had organized some of the early low-dosage methadone clinics in the 1960s. We had lunch at a restaurant on Charlotte Street—Bordeaux pigeon, little peas, and a bottle of claret—and talked about his research in the pharmacology of LSD. Dr. Freedman said, "The reason I'm interested in drugs, they're the greatest moral tale we've got, at the moment, to make people think about the complexity of the interactions through which society organizes our behavior.")

One man who completely reverses the all but universal rejection of heroin by the American medical profession is Elmer Gardner, who was head of the Division of Neuropharmacological Drug Products in the Food and Drug Administration until February 1974, and thus was one of the pivotal people for federal approval of any American experiment with heroin maintenance. Dr. Gardner came to Washington in 1970 from community mental-health work—what he calls "psychiatric epidemiology"—in Philadelphia. "Yes, I think heroin maintenance will be tried in the United States, at least experimentally," Gardner said, several months after the Vera Institute published its proposal. "The only reason we in this agency would have for stopping it would be lack of safety of the drug. Beyond experiment, I can only give you my own opinion. First of all, I don't see any harm in people having drugs for pleasure, even if the drugs are addictive, unless they have degenerative effects as well. About heroin, the things we really don't know are in the realm of chronic toxicity—for example, carcinogenic effects or liver damage—with long-term use. There have not even been good chronic-effect *animal* studies with heroin. Heroin is probably—but we don't know—physically less damaging than alcohol. Given that reservation, my feeling is that if someone needs heroin enough to get addicted, then he probably ought to be able to get it. It may sound strange coming from a psychiatrist, but I don't see this entirely as a matter of treating illness. I guess my answer is, yes, we do need heroin maintenance—in addition to methadone, and for some people, anyway. At least until we come up with something better, and by that I mean something better for pleasure and the relief of anxiety and all the rest of it."

Probably no English doctor, or none I've met, would go so far. The English doctors see every day the real nature of heroin, as no American physician can—its benefits and drawbacks, whether in general medical use or in the management of addiction. Even those who prefer to prescribe heroin for addicts will say, as Martin Mitcheson did, "My personal feeling is that heroin is far too powerful a drug ever to leave to normal social controls. I'm perfectly able to accept the idea that to a heroin addict heroin is such a rewarding drug that he is prepared to ruin every aspect of his life to get it."

I asked Dr. Mitcheson what he had seen in the States that he wanted to take back with him to England. "I am concerned, personally, to see people get free of drugs," he said.

"Some people here obviously get virtually free of drugs through methadone programs; these people I would guess are the more stable addicts, anyway. But apart from them I think there are people who need a therapeutic community of some sort—who need a much more radical reprograming." There are only four such communities for ex-addicts in England; they all derive directly and without real innovation from the early American model, Phoenix House. The British concede that in this approach to treatment of addiction the Americans are far ahead. Mitcheson described therapeutic methods and attitudes, new to him, that interested him very much in communities he had visited in San Francisco, the Bronx, and Washington. "There are little things I want to take back with me, too," he then said. "Like the idea of prescribing Antabuse plus Librium for the alcoholic, which is a mixture the Chicago clinics have had to develop; they've got a considerable alcohol problem amongst their people on stable methadone doses. As they do in New York. Nowhere that I saw has anybody yet acquired our English addicts' habit of injecting barbiturates; so everyone working in drugs just denied that this was any kind of a problem, and I found myself wanting to say, 'Well, wait and see.' I tried to take a few bets on that, and I'm not a betting man. My belief about that is that if the Bureau of Narcotics maintains the pressure there's been recently on the heroin supply, and the local police keep stepping up the pressure on the addicts' financial resources—then the addict will either find himself in prison or, at a certain level of difficulty in making money, he will come into the methadone program. And what then? If he's taking his regular methadone, and wants to get something more? We're talking about somebody who has experimented with drugs anyway, and likes their effects, for whatever reason, whether it was self-medication of anxiety or for sheer hedonism, to which you must add the

powerful reinforcing, conditioning effects of the drug use itself. So: I can't believe that solving the opiate aspect of the
junkie's life—whether it's your methadone or our heroin, mind
you—is going to cure everything. I think you are still left on
the one hand with the environmental and societal problems.
And on the other hand you're left with the conditioned addiction, as well as whatever psychopathology may have been
troubling the person before he ever took drugs—and those two,
I think, are the proper province of the doctor and his colleagues. But methadone or legal heroin—neither is going to
solve the psychopathology. So I would anticipate that as your
programs begin to look again at the quality of what they are
doing, and at the extent of multiple-drug use, and as the
addicts learn to look, still more, for what's available elsewhere—even if it's eventually only alcohol, in that distant day
after amphetamines and then barbiturates have been removed
from the pharmacopeia—then I think you'll see that the drug
problem has changed, in some ways for the worse, but has
not gone away. Whether, and to what extent, these multiple-
drug users will be stealing and robbing in order to get the
drugs to get high, or whether they will just be skid-row char-
acters who need to be segregated out of the sight of the middle-
class eye, I don't know. After all, alcohol is still a much greater
problem—in your country as well as mine—in terms of personal
damage, than heroin has ever been. Perhaps the problem will
not be sufficiently disturbing to produce the funds. And that,
I suppose, if I were a betting man, and were putting something into an envelope to be opened in three years' time, that
I think is what I'd say."

(At that same drugs conference in London, I talked for a
few minutes—over instant coffee and digestive biscuits—with
Richard Blum, who had flown in from Stanford to present a
paper on the international approach to drug problems. As we

got up to go back to the auditorium, Dr. Blum said, "Drugs
seem to be the final path of expression for almost any other
social problem—poverty, race, families, social class. Drugs,
I've come to think, are the chemical tracer that diagnoses the
problems of society. An avenue of discovery for the doctor
and the sociologist.")

The conversation with Mitcheson turned to the problem of
doctors being used as agents of social control. "I had a session the other day with a man who runs a methadone program
near here," Mitcheson said. "He's a young, suave doctor, I
should think a liberal Republican, talks about himself as being
'essentially a bureaucrat.' On the defensive. When I mentioned that I saw the methadone programs as a useful way to
reduce crime, he started insisting that he was a doctor running
a medical service, and crime was up to the police. So I asked
him why, then, did he have that graph on his wall with two
lines on it, one for the number of people in the methadone
programs, going up, and the other for the crime figures, coming down. And you know, the question bothered him—'That's
not claiming that the methadone's doing it,' he said. But let's
be clear about it, this really is part of the job that the doctors
have been asked to do. Of course we have our own way of
going at it. But the only honest thing is to say, well, we *are*
agents of social control. Among other things. But I don't find
it difficult to justify this in terms of what happens to the
individual if this form of behavior is not controlled. There
is a very long tradition, in my view, of doctors being concerned with the public health."

As I hope I have conveyed, the problem of heroin addiction feels very different in England from the way it feels in
the United States. I have talked with many English addicts
over the past eight years. They are ridden by numberless petty

dreads and hopes, as addicts seem to be everywhere. The old
street junkies are indeed very far down; the automaton that
we know lives in each of us has taken them over. The young
ones may be cocky, but more often they seem very tired.
Grudgingly, they admit that they like the clinics and feel safe
there. "S'awright. 'Course, they never give you enough." They
all claim that they supplement their clinic prescriptions with
Chinese heroin. But then it is in their interest—about this they
have a tacit but real alliance with the Home Office Drugs
Branch—to persuade the clinic doctors that suppression of the
black market requires that the tap be eased open on legal
narcotics. Along the two blocks of Gerrard Street, the Chinese-
restaurant quarter that has grown up at the southern edge of
Soho, there is never the action you will see at any time on a
New York corner like Broadway and Ninety-sixth Street. Indeed, on Gerrard Street at midnight the loudest sound is the
click of mah-jongg tiles.

In the waiting room of Dr. Mitcheson's clinic at University
College Hospital, I met an addict who has remained in my
mind more than any other. He said that his problem was
insomnia, and that his wife had the same trouble, and that
the last thing at night they used their methadone syrup so
they could get to sleep. He called across the room to a staff
member for a supply of sterile disposable syringes. "Twenty-
one, please—seven for my wife, fourteen for me. Don't worry
about the swabs, we got plenty of swabs." Then he told me
he was afraid of losing his job. What did he do? "I'm a fish-
monger." Addict braggadocio. He was in fact a kitchen helper
who killed the lobsters and crabs at one of London's oyster
houses. He had held the job nearly nine months. Now he had
begun to nod off at work. And he thought his boss had noticed
a needle that had failed to flush down the employee toilet.
And blood on the towel. His despair was terrible. But it was

uniquely personal. An American addict would find it unrecognizably innocent.

Does the British approach to heroin addiction work? In the light of the inherent instability of the drug situation in every Western country, I think it has worked very well—for the British. Credit for limiting the epidemic, however, can hardly be given simply to the clinics' prescribing of narcotics. Once again, the medical model, though an improvement on enforcement and punishment, is not enough. Any explanation of what has happened with heroin in England needs to begin with the worldwide phenomenon of the 1960s: the coming of age of the children born—in such disproportionate numbers as to strain the social fabric—just after the Second World War. Behind all the teen-age phenomena so often described and imperfectly explained, there was an evident shift in the adolescents' axis of relationships: their lives became much less tied to their parents' generation, and much more strongly controlled by their own age group. We think of the continuity of generations as characterized by rebellion—not by indifference on such a scale. Now, part of the pleasure of living in England in the 1960s was the emergent youth. The delight was greater because of the most considerable difference between the English adolescent mood and the American, which was a quality of ease. One was told many times, "The Beatles—ah, yes, d'you see, the mums love them, too." The mothers did. "The working-class lad may have his mod clothes and hair to his shoulders, but Saturday night you'll find him drinking in the pub with his dad, short-back-and-sides, in his Burton suit," I was told, and that was true, too. Across the gap there was an unexpected degree of tolerance. If it was simple-minded to blame the English heroin epidemic on the overprescribing general practitioners, alone, it must be inadequate to credit the remission in the epidemic solely to the introduction of the clinics. At least as important was the particular continuity that life, the social fabric, was felt to have by the adolescents who drew back from addiction. So much for conjecture.

What everybody knows about the British and heroin is that they supply it on prescription to heroin addicts. The common knowledge obscures the fact that, in the years since the clinics opened, their aims have changed. The doctors have quietly refused to remain merely agents of social control: though they recognize the role, and acknowledge there are addicts whose addiction can only be supported, the clinic staffs have gradually come to have a commitment to the eventual integration of the addict into the community, and to the diminution of doses. In this fundamental respect, the English approach to heroin maintenance is the reverse of the surrender that many Americans take it to be.

In 1971, after a decline the year before, the total number of addicts of all kinds of narcotics who were known to the Home Office rose again, for the entire year cumulatively, to 2,769. Still, this was lower than the figure for the peak year, 1969. But in 1972 the total number rose to 2,944, the highest yet recorded. As before, there is a second set of index figures, for the last day of each year. On 31 December 1971, 1,555 addicts of all kinds of narcotics were known, which was also an increase; at the end of 1972, this figure had climbed to 1,619. The total number addicted to heroin or methadone or both remained fairly steady for three years—2,480 throughout 1969, 2,233 in 1970, 2,376 in 1971—but on 31 December 1971, there were believed to be 1,316 addicts of those two alternative drugs, and a year later, 1,418, which was the highest year-end figure yet. In 1971, for the first time since the clinics opened, the number addicted to heroin alone rose also, though only from 413 to 449; in 1972 this number dropped back slightly to 442. The number of addicts less than twenty years old has gone down every year since the peak in 1968, so that by 1972 there were just over one-third as many teen-age addicts as there had been four years earlier. Statistics for 1973 had not been released by 15 July 1974, but the figures will show an increase in the total number of addicts of all narcotics at the end of the year—up from 1,619 at the end of 1972 to about eighteen hundred on 31 December 1973. Yet in 1973, notifications to the Home Office of *new* cases of heroin addiction ran somewhat lower than the year before. The increase in the total was in great part due to old addicts returning to the clinics, whose rosters showed a parallel rise in the year. The situation still seems almost stable.

Does the British approach work? The British themselves have a wary confidence that it does. "Nonetheless, I think my overriding concern would be to avoid answering that question," Griffith Edwards said at the end of lunch. "One would be quite foolish to invest all one's pride and all one's cleverness in defense of one particular medicine—or system. The numbers game. How precise must the data be for intelligent policy making? And what *is* 'the size of the problem'—simply its numerical dimensions, or the dimensions of the anxiety it generates? My impression is that the anxiety about narcotics here is surprisingly low. Just about right, in fact."

Just about right. In the course of a conversation I had at yet another English drug-dependence clinic, a doctor said something in passing that seemed so natural that it was an hour later, as I was boarding a train in the London Underground, that I woke to what he had said, and to what an overturning of my American expectations it represented. The doctor told me, "We have made it possible in this city for the addict to live without fear."

Statistical Appendix

The following tables are compiled from four sources:

Great Britain, Home Office, *Report to the United Nations by Her Majesty's Government in the United Kingdom . . . on the Traffic in Opium and Other Dangerous Drugs, for 1954,* and *Report to the United Nations by Her Majesty's Government . . . on the Working of the International Treaties on Narcotic Drugs,* 1955 and every year through 1972.

Great Britain, Home Office, "United Kingdom Statistics of Drug Addiction and Criminal Offences Involving Drugs" (London: Home Office, issued annually and cumulatively), 1973.

H. B. Spear, "The Growth of Heroin Addiction in the United Kingdom," *British Journal of Addiction* 64 (1969): 247, 250.

Great Britain, Department of Health and Social Security, *Annual Report* (London: HMSO), 1969, Table 81, pp. 283–84; 1970, Table 80, p. 299; 1971, p. 56.

Statistics for 1973 were not released by 15 July 1974.

HEROIN ADDICTION IN BRITAIN: A. THE INDEX THROUGH 1968

United Kingdom

	1945	1953	1954	1955	1956	1957	1958	1959	1960	1961	1962	1963	1964	1965	1966	1967	1968
Addicts known																	
all narcotics	367	290	317	335	333	359	442	454	437	470	532	635	753	927	1,349	1,729	2,782
male	144	149	148	159	163	174	197	196	195	223	262	339	409	558	886	1,262	2,161
female	223	141	169	176	170	185	245	258	242	247	270	296	344	369	463	467	621
taking heroin [1]			**57**	**54**	**53**	**66**	**62**	**68**	**94**	**132**	**175**	**237**	**342**	**521**	**899**	**1,299**	**2,240**
taking methadone —but not heroin [1]				21	20	31	47	58	68	59	54[b]	59[b]	62	62	156	243	486
									67	58	51	55	54	61	74	102	196
taking cocaine [2]				6	6	16	25	30	52	84	112	171	211	311	443	462	564
taking morphine				179	176	178	205	204	177	168	157	172	162	160	178	158	198
Origin of addiction																	
"therapeutic," [3] all drugs							349	344	309	293	312	355	368	344	351	313	306
heroin addicts			20	18	17	21	19	21	22	20	18	15	13	12	13	9	8
not therapeutic, all drugs							68	98	122	159	212	270	372	580	982	1,385	2,420
heroin addicts			**37**	**36**	**36**	**45**	**43**	**47**	**72**	**112**	**157**	**222**	**329**	**509**	**885**	**1,290**	**2,232**
origin unknown							25	12	6	18	8	10	13	3	16	31	56
doctors, dentists, pharmacists, nurses	80	71	72	86[a]	99	88	74	68	63	61	57	56	58	45	54	56	43
Changes in index																	
addicts added, all drugs				50	42	90	104	130	98	137	169	235	263	351	662	696	1,539
recidivists				4	3	6	5	13	10	8	10	26	17	19	29	32	63
new cases				46	39	84	99	117	88	129	159	209	246	332	633	664	1,476
heroin addicts added	**1**	**4**	**18**	**10**	**10**	**7**	**11**	**11**	**24**	**56**	**72**	**90**	**162**	**259**	**522**	**745**	**1,306**
therapeutic origin	1		2	1	1	2	3	2	1	2	2		2		3		2
dropped, all drugs							21	118	115	104	107	132	145	177	242	316	486
"considered cured" [4]							11	77	69	51	61	62	83	114	156	102	152
died							10	40	36	32	34	39	36	29	44	37	47
disappeared								1	10	21	12	31	26	34	40	177	287

The Home Office's grand total across the top line includes people who were addicted to morphine, pethidine, dextromoramide, and other drugs, natural or synthetic, related to morphine; most of these cases originated in medical treatment for something other than addiction. Before the late 1960s, methadone was used primarily as one of these synthetic alternatives to morphine or heroin in medical practice rather than as a treatment or substitute for heroin addiction.

[1] Drugs used alone or in combination with other narcotics: an addict using several drugs will be counted under each.

[2] Almost all cocaine addicts also used heroin.

[3] Therapeutic: that is, an addiction that arose in the course of medical treatment for some other condition.

[4] "Considered cured": including those not known to be taking drugs that year, whether or not they had been in treatment for addiction.

[a] Includes nurses for the first time.

[b] As reported to United Nations; Home Office cumulative tables show 55 methadone addicts in 1962 and 61 in 1963.

HEROIN ADDICTION IN BRITAIN: B. 1967–1973
1. Addicts, Drugs

United Kingdom

Addicts	1967 full year	1968 full year	1969 full year	1969 on 12/31	1970 full year	1970 on 12/31	1971 full year	1971 on 12/31	1972 full year	1972 on 12/31	1973 full year on 12/31
of all narcotics	**1,729**	**2,782**[a]	**2,881**	**1,466**	**2,661**	**1,430**	**2,769**	**1,555**	**2,944**	**1,619**	not available by 15 July 1974
male	1,262	2,161	2,295	1,067	2,071	1,053	2,134	1,135	2,272	1,197	
female	467	621	586	399	590	377	635	420	672	422	
taking heroin[1]	1,299	2,240	1,417	499	914	437	959	385	868	339	
—but not methadone	1,158	1,950	793	204	413	183	449	156	442	138	
male			672	155		135		119		99	
female			121	49		48		37		39	
taking methadone	243	486	1,687	1,011	1,820	992	1,927	1,160	2,171	1,280	
—but not heroin	102	196	1,063	716	1,319	738	1,417	931	1,745	1,079	
male			1,387	801		792		913		1,014	
female			300	210		200		247		266	
taking heroin or methadone or both	**1,401**	**2,436**	**2,480**	**1,215**	**2,233**	**1,175**	**2,376**	**1,316**	**2,613**	**1,418**	
male			2,059	956		927		1,032		1,113	
female			421	259		248		284		305	
taking cocaine	462	564	311	81	198	57	178	58	178	46	
taking morphine	158	198	345	111	346	105	346	103	292	90	
taking pethidine	112	120	128	83	122	80	135	73	98	59	
Notifications in year											
all addicts notified by physicians[2]		1,539	1,135		1,195		1,339		1,388		
recidivists		63	103		484		562		587		
new cases		1,476	1,030		711		777		801		
heroin addicts							531		510		
recidivists							184		189		
new cases							347		321		
methadone addicts							636		760		
recidivists							345		372		
new cases							291		388		

[1] Drugs used alone or in combination with other narcotics; an addict using several drugs will be included under each. The widespread use of methadone as a treatment for heroin addiction began in the late 1960s, when, therefore, the number of addicts of heroin or methadone or both becomes the inclusive indicator of the extent of addiction as a problem in public health. This figure should be compared with that for "non-therapeutic" addicts in Part 2 of this table.

[2] Beginning on 22 February 1968, doctors were required by law to notify the Home Office of any case in which addiction was suspected; compulsory notification changed the basis of the statistics, so that this line is not strictly comparable to "addicts added" to index in the previous section of this table.

[a] The Home Office also reported to the United Nations that on 31 December 1968 there were 1,746 known addicts of all narcotics and cocaine.

2. Origins of Addiction

United Kingdom

Origin	1967 full year	1968 full year	1969 full year	1969 on 12/31	1970 full year	1970 on 12/31	1971 full year	1971 on 12/31	1972 full year	1972 on 12/31	1973 full year	1973 on 12/31
All addicts, all narcotics	1,729	2,782	2,881	1,466	2,661	1,430	2,769	1,555	2,944	1,619	not available by 15 July 1974	
therapeutic,[1] all narc.	313	306	289	247	295	231	265	218	244	180		
heroin								5		3		
methadone								30		25		
not therapeutic, all narc.	1,385	2,420	2,533	1,196	2,321	1,177	2,457	1,313	2,659	1,413		
heroin								375		331		
methadone								877		1,024		
origin unknown	31	56	59	23	45	22	47	24	41	26		
doctors, dentists, nurses, pharmacists	56	43	43	26	38	26	44	22	33	23		

[1] A case of addiction is "therapeutic" in origin when it has arisen in the course of medical treatment for something else.

3. Addicts in Treatment

England

Number in treatment at year end	1968	1969	1970	1971	1972	1973
	1,242	1,235	1,253	1,145	1,361	1,506
as inpatients	103	91	122	58	73	64
as outpatients	1,139	1,144	1,131	1,087	1,288	1,442

CRIMINAL CONVICTIONS FOR OFFENSES INVOLVING DRUGS

United Kingdom

Convictions for offenses involving—	1945	1954	1956	1958	1960	1961	1962	1963	1964	1965	1966	1967	1968	1969	1970	1971	1972	1973
opium	206	28	12	8	15	15	16	20	14	13	36	58	73	53	66	55	98	[a]
cannabis (total)	**4**	**144**	**103**	**99**	**235**	**288**	**588**	**663**	**544**	**626**	**1,119**	**2,393**	**3,071**	**4,683**	**7,520**	**9,219**	**12,365**	
unlawful possession			97			278	558	650	532	610	1,083	2,193	2,663	4,094	6,545	7,837	10,986	
unlawful import			5			10	29	13	12	4	10	37	77	122	171	224	243	
manufactured drugs [1] (total)	20	28	37	41	26	61	71	63	101	128	242	573	1,099	1,359	1,214	1,570	2,068	
heroin												**274**	**539**	**341**	**281**	**580**	**665**	
unlawful possession												213	391	200	157	439	471	
unlawful import												2	0	1	1	0	1	
unlawful supply												20	41	36	20	54	33	
unlawful procuring												13	36	26	9	15	20	
larceny												14	33	77	93	71	134	
other												12	38	1	1	1	6	
cocaine												86	111	140	162	126	245	

[1] Morphine and derivatives, related synthetics, cocaine.
[a] Not available by 15 July 1974.

161

Notes

Along that contentious border where journalism marches with historical research, some problems of citation are presented by interviews. The problems are of two kinds: accuracy and attribution. I tape-record interviews when possible, and always transcribe the tapes myself. In a few instances, interviews were taken down in notebooks, in a condensed longhand; I try to type out the notes the same day. Nothing appears within quotation marks except the words of my respondent that I actually recorded or took down; I have sometimes supplied his antecedent or elided a repetition or a self-correction, but I do even that kind of editing rarely. Several people, including some of the best informed, had to ask that their statements not be attributed to them, or not even to their organizations. British civil servants are bound by this sort of rule, as was an official at a manufacturing concern. Therefore, some apparently fatherless entries in my text will have to prove their pedigrees in the running.

The interviews from which I used quotations or information were conducted as follows, and will be cited further in these notes only when the text does not identify an important source (or make clear the date of the conversation, where relevant).

Don Aitken, of Release, London, September 1972 and December 1973

Dr. Thomas Bewley, Lambeth Hospital, London, August 1972; some details rechecked, January 1973 and April 1974.

Professor Richard Blum, Stanford University, interviews in London, April 1973, and Washington, D.C., September 1973

Dr. Thomas Bryant, Drug Abuse Council, interview in New York City, July 1972

Dr. Peter A. L. Chapple, National Addiction Research Institute, London, July 1972

Dr. Philip Connell, The Bethlem Royal Hospital, London, August 1972; rechecked with him.

Department of Health and Social Security, London, various informants, August 1972, January and April 1973

Dr. Griffith Edwards, Addiction Research Unit, Institute of Psychiatry, The Maudsley Hospital, London, August 1972 and December 1973

Graham Finney, New York, June 1972, when he was commissioner of New York City's Addiction Services Agency

Professor Daniel X. Freedman, University of Chicago, interviews in London, April 1973, and Chicago, October 1973

Dr. Elmer Gardner, Food and Drug Administration, Rockville, Maryland, July 1972; rechecked with him.

Dr. Max Glatt, editor, *British Journal of Addiction*, London, September 1972

Dr. David Hawks, Addiction Research Unit, Institute of Psychiatry, London, January 1973

Edward David Hill, All Saints' Hospital, Birmingham, August 1972

Home Office, London, various informants, August, September, and December 1972; January, August, and October 1973; May 1974

Commander Robert Huntley, Metropolitan Police, New Scotland Yard, London, January 1973

Dr. Ian Pierce James, Glenside Hospital, Bristol, August 1972 and November 1973

Rt. Hon. Roy Jenkins, M.P., House of Commons, London, January 1973; rechecked with him.

Dr. John Mack, Miss Susan Norvill, Hackney Hospital, London, August 1972

Dr. Martin Mitcheson, University College Hospital, interviews in London, August 1972, rechecked with him, and in Washington, D.C., March 1973.

Dr. Robert Newman, New York City, June 1972

Dr. Gisela Brigitte Oppenheim, Charing Cross Hospital, London, August 1972; rechecked with her.

Hon. Charles Rangel, House of Representatives, interview in New York City, June 1972

Colin Roberts, Addiction Research Unit, Institute of Psychiatry, London, September 1973

Dr. Margaret Tripp, interviews in Colchester, August 1972, and Washington, D.C., March 1973

Dr. James Willis, St. Giles' Hospital, London, April 1973

Jim Zacune, North Staffordshire Polytechnic, Stoke-on-Trent, interview in London, September 1972

Dr. Norman Zinberg, Cambridge, Mass., interviews in England, August 1972, and Cambridge, Mass., October 1973

SOURCES

v

the epigraph: Griffith Edwards, "Drug Problems UK/USA," *Anglo-American Conference on Drug Abuse: Proceedings of a Conference Sponsored Jointly by the Royal Society of Medicine and the Royal Society of Medicine Foundation, Inc., 16–18 April 1973,* ed. R. A. Bowen (London: Royal Society of Medicine, 1973), p. 2.

4

1874: C. R. A. Wright, "On the Action of Organic Acids and Their Anhydrides on the Natural Alkaloïds. Part I," *Journal of the Chemical Society* 27 (1874):1031, 1037.

4

1898: H. Dreser, "Pharmakologisches über einige Morphinderivate," *Therapeutische Monatshefte* 12 (September 1898):509–512; Floret, "Klinische Versuche über die Wirkung und Anwendung des Heroins," ibid., 512; H. Dreser, "Pharmakologisches über Aspirin (Acetylsalicylsäure)," *Archiv für die Gesammte Physiologie* 76 (1899):306 and n.

4

Congress of Naturalists: reported in *Journal of the American Medical Association* 31 (12 November 1898):1176.

5

other clinicians: e.g., Morris Manges, *New York Medical Journal*
    68 (26 November 1898):768–770; and *Lancet* 1898 (2) (3
    December):1511, (24 December):1744.

5

call for English tests: Lancet 1898 (2) (3 December):1486.

5–7

lawful heroin: United Nations, International Narcotics Control
    Board, *Estimated World Requirements of Narcotic Drugs
    and Estimates of World Production of Opium in 1974*
    (E/INCB/22) (New York: United Nations, 1973), passim.

5–6

chemistry: Wright, "On the Action of Organic Acids," p. 1037;
    Arthur Osol and Robertson Pratt, eds., *The United States Dis-
    pensatory,* 27th ed. (Philadelphia: J. B. Lippincott Co., 1973),
    p. 409; *British Pharmacopoeia 1973* (London: HMSO, 1973),
    entries for diamorphine hydrochloride, p. 153, morphine sul-
    phate, pp. 310–311; Pharmaceutical Society of Great Britain,
    Martindale: The Extra Pharmacopoeia, 26th ed., ed. Norman
    W. Blacow (London: Pharmaceutical Press, 1972), pp. 1100,
    1114–1116; Lyndon F. Small and Robert E. Lutz, *Chemistry
    of the Opium Alkaloids,* Supplement 103 to the Public Health
    Reports (Washington: Government Printing Office, 1932), pp.
    146, 153–154; Roger Lewin, "A Step Towards Safer Mor-
    phine," *New Scientist* 61 (10 January 1974):64–65.

6

fifty million dollars: see, e.g., John F. Holahan, "The Economics of
    Heroin," *Dealing with Drug Abuse: A Report to the Ford
    Foundation* (New York: Praeger, 1972), p. 290; and Edward
    A. Preble and John J. Casey, Jr., "Taking Care of Business—
    the Heroin User's Life on the Street," *International Journal
    of the Addictions* 4 (March 1969):8.

7

neurobiology: G. Manner, F. F. Foldes, Marilyn Kuleba, and
    Ann M. Deery, "Morphine Tolerance in a Human Neuro-
    blastoma Line," *Experientia* 30 (1974):137–138; Michael J.
    Kuhar, Candace B. Pert, and Solomon H. Snyder, "Regional

Distribution of Opiate Receptor Binding in Monkey and Human Brain," *Nature* 245 (26 October 1973):447–450; Candace B. Pert, Gavril Pasternak, and Solomon H. Snyder, "Opiate Agonists and Antagonists Discriminated by Receptor Binding in Brain," *Science* 182 (28 December 1973):1359–1361; Louise I. Lowney, Karin Schulz, Patricia Lowery, and Avram Goldstein, "Partial Purification of an Opiate Receptor from Mouse Brain," *Science* 183 (22 February 1974):749–753.

8–9

heroin in British medicine: Pharmaceutical Society, *Martindale,* pp. 1114–1116; Stanley Alstead, "Analgesics and Hypnotics," *Textbook of Medical Treatment,* 12th ed., eds. Stanley Alstead, Alastair G. Macgregor, and Ronald H. Girdwood (Edinburgh and London: Churchill Livingstone, 1971), pp. 442–443. See also references cited for the controversy in 1955, over possible discontinuance of heroin production, below, note to pp. 29–30.

8

heroin and cancer: C. Saunders, "The Treatment of Intractable Pain in Terminal Cancer," *Proceedings of the Royal Society of Medicine* 56 (1963):195–197; Cicely Saunders, *The Management of Terminal Illness* (London: Hospital Medical Publications, 1967), pp. 17, 18; R. G. Twycross, "Principles and Practice in the Relief of Pain in Terminal Cancer," *Update* (London) 5 (July 1972):117–118.

9

heroin and coronaries: H. R. MacDonald, H. A. Rees, A. L. Muir, D. M. Lawrie, J. L. Burton, and K. W. Donald, "Circulatory Effects of Heroin in Patients with Myocardial Infarction," *Lancet* 1967 (1):1070–1074. Interviews, Home Office, August 1972, and with British physicians at various times.

9

heroin and surgery: C. W. Reichle, G. M. Smith, J. S. Gravenstein, S. G. Macris, and H. K. Beecher, "Comparative Analgesic Potency of Heroin and Morphine in Postoperative Patients," *Journal of Pharmacology and Experimental Therapeutics* 136 (1962):43–46; Pharmaceutical Society, *Martindale,* p. 1115.

9

heroin and shingles: Henry Miller, *Medicine and Society* (London: Oxford University Press, 1973), p. 9.

11

Vera Institute's proposal: analysis and comparison with the British approach to heroin addiction, below, part 3, pp. 126–139. Staff of the Vera Institute of Justice prepared a memorandum, *Heroin Research and Research and Rehabilitation Program* (New York: Vera Institute of Justice, Inc., May 1971); a year later, a reworked version was made public: Charles E. Riordan and Leroy C. Gould, *Proposal for the Use of Diacetyl Morphine (Heroin) in the Treatment of Heroin Dependent Individuals* (New York: Vera Institute of Justice, Inc., May 1972). For the controversy aroused by the proposal, and the idea of "treatment lure," see James M. Markham, "What's All This Talk of Heroin Maintenance?" *The New York Times Magazine*, 2 July 1972, p. 6 et seq.

11

legal heroin and crime: see, e.g., Norval Morris, "Crimes Without Victims," *The New York Times Magazine*, 1 April 1973, p. 10 et seq., particularly pp. 59–60.

11

U.K. addiction statistics: table, below, p. 159.

11

U.S. addiction statistics: these vary, depending on the source as well as the year. Mid-1972, the Bureau of Narcotics and Dangerous Drugs estimated 565,000 addicts in the United States (confirmed by conversation with press office); a similar figure, 560,000 appears in a paper by an employee of B.N.D.D., Edward Lewis, Jr., "A Heroin Maintenance Program in the United States?" *Journal of the American Medical Association* 223 (29 January 1973):546. Yet, in January 1973, the B.N.D.D. revised its estimate to 626,000 addicts in the United States (confirmed by telephone with B.N.D.D. in June 1973). The New York City figures are from interviews in June 1972 with Graham Finney and Robert Newman, medical director of the city's methadone programs; these numbers, too, were rechecked in June 1973. See also, e.g., Graham S. Finney and Raymond H. Godfrey, Jr., "Heroin Addiction and Drug Abuse in New York," *City Almanac* 6 (April 1972):3; and the letter to the editor of *The New York Times* by Norman E. Zinberg and Charles E. Riordan, 23 June 1972, p. 36.

12

Griffith Edwards: interview, August 1972, Institute of Psychiatry, London.

13

policemen and missionaries: one recent book supersedes other sources: David F. Musto, *The American Disease: Origins of Narcotics Control* (New Haven and London: Yale University Press, 1973), pp. 25–40, 49–53.

14

Harrison Act: United States, Public Acts of the Sixty-third Congress, P.L. 223, "An Act to provide for the registration of, with collectors of internal revenue, and to impose a special tax upon all persons who produce, import, manufacture, compound, deal in, dispense, sell, distribute, or give away opium or coca leaves, their salts, derivatives, or preparations, and for other purposes," 63rd Cong., 3rd sess., 17 December 1914.

14

a dollar a year: ibid., Sec. 1.

14

legitimate practice, good faith: ibid., Sec. 2, Sec. 8; Musto, *The American Disease,* p. 125.

14–15

regulations and court decisions: Charles E. Terry and Mildred Pellens, *The Opium Problem* (New York: Bureau of Social Hygiene, 1928), pp. 753–770; Musto, *The American Disease,* pp. 63–68, 121–150.

15

medical protests: e.g., *Illinois Medical Journal* 30 (August 1916): 143–144; *New York Medical Journal* 103 (27 May 1916): 1036; *Medical Record,* New York 99 (1 January 1921):18, 20.

15

U.S. clinics: Musto, *The American Disease,* pp. 140–141, 147–182.

15

structure of treaties: United Nations, Office of Public Information, *The United Nations and the Fight Against Drug Abuse* (New York: United Nations, 1972), pp. 7–15.

16

two federal acts of 1970: Lorrin M. Koran, "Heroin Maintenance for Heroin Addicts: Issues and Evidence," *New England Journal of Medicine* 288 (29 March 1973):655–656; John Ruhnka, "Legal Authorization," Appendix B in Riordan and Gould, *Vera Institute Proposal,* pp. B1–B2. Interview, Elmer Gardner.

16

secret tussle: G. F. McLeary, Ministry of Health, to Sir Malcolm Delevingne, Home Office, 27 June 1919; Delevingne to McLeary, 7 July 1919, Great Britain, Public Record Office, quoted in Edwards, "Drug Problems UK/USA," p. 5.

17

Dangerous Drugs Act, 1920: 10 & 11 Geo. 5, Ch. 46.

17

Home Office and prohibition: Edwards, "Drug Problems UK/USA," p. 5, gives information from archives not yet public, but which I have been able to verify independently; see also Great Britain, Ministry of Health, *Departmental Committee on Morphine and Heroin Addiction, 1926,* the Report of the Rolleston Committee (London: HMSO, 1926), p. 7, where the Home Office view (which was in fact Delevingne's strong personal conviction) is discussed. (Cited henceforth as Rolleston, *Report.*)

17–18

debate: Great Britain, *Parliamentary Debates* (Commons), 5th ser., 130 (1920):723.

18

Campbell's trip: Harry Campbell, "The Pathology and Treatment of Morphia Addiction," *British Journal of Inebriety* 20 (April 1923): 150–151.

18–19

strength of medical profession: see, e.g., Michael Foot, 2 vols. *Aneurin Bevan,* vol. 2 (London: Davis-Poynter, 1973), pp. 137, 152, 188–189.

19

British medical opinion: e.g., in a memorandum prepared by medical advisers to the Ministry of Health and transmitted, with comments, in a letter from G. F. McLeary of the Ministry of Health to Delevingne, Home Office, 5 March 1923.

19–20

Rolleston: obituary, *Lancet* 1944 (2) (7 October):487–488; L. G. Wickham Legg and E. T. Williams, eds., *The Dictionary of National Biography, 1941–1950* (London: Oxford University Press, 1959), pp. 733–734.

20

central issue: Rolleston, *Report,* p. 7.

21

committee's conclusion (the stable addict): ibid., p. 18.

21

weakness and surrender: speech by John E. Ingersoll, Director, Bureau of Narcotics and Dangerous Drugs, to the California Peace Officers Association, Anaheim, California, 24 May 1972; text from B.N.D.D.

22

prosecutions in 1925: H. B. Spear, "The Growth of Heroin Addiction in the United Kingdom," *British Journal of Addiction* 64 (1969):246, table 1.

22–23

two issues of administration: Rolleston, *Report,* pp. 24–26.

23

confusion and Consumers Union: Edward M. Brecher and the

editors of Consumer Reports, *Licit and Illicit Drugs: The Consumers Union Report* (Boston: Little, Brown, 1972), p. 177.

25

1936 and later statistics: Spear, "Growth of Heroin Addiction," p. 247, table 2a.

27

addicts in 1950: ibid.; interviews, Home Office, August and December 1972.

28

"Mark": Spear, "Growth of Heroin Addiction," p. 251, where, however, he gets the date of the burglary wrong. Saunders came to trial 17 October 1951, and was sentenced to two years in prison: London *Evening News,* 17 October; *Daily Mirror,* 19 October; *Express,* 19 October; *News of the World,* 20 October 1951.

28

six Nigerians: Spear, "Growth of Heroin Addiction," lists five, but six is correct (Spear, personal communication, July 1973).

29

Lloyd-George's announcement: Great Britain, *Parliamentary Debates* (Commons), 5th ser., 537 (1955), "Written Answers to Questions," col. 94. The ensuing controversy was extensively covered in *The British Medical Journal, The Lancet,* and *The Times.* I have verified details and added others through interviews and from cabled reports to *Time* magazine from the London bureau of the Time-Life News Service in December 1955. See, in particular, *Lancet* 1955 (1):965, 1218, 1227, 1271, 1277–1278, 1311–1312 (leading article with thorough recapitulation); and *Lancet* 1955 (2):148, 1143, 1180–1181 (another summary of events), 1183–1184, 1250–1252 (the penultimate parliamentary debates, but confusing about dates), 1333–1335 (climax in House of Lords).

29–30

U.S. pressure through U.N.: conversation, Sir Harry Greenfield,

president, International Narcotics Control Board of the United
Nations, in London, April 1973; *Lancet* 1955 (1):1277; *Lancet*
1955 (2):1180–1181, 1183–1184.

30

drift of medical opinion: Lancet 1955 (1):1311–1312; *Lancet* 1955
(2):148, 1183–1184. *British Pharmacopoeia 1953:* no entry for
diamorphine.

31

pains, stockpiling: The Times, 19 November 1955, p. 6; 23 November, p. 10, and letters.

32

newspapers: The Times, 1 December 1955, first leader.

32

Macleod: Parliamentary Debates (Commons), 5th ser., 547
(1955):27.

32

Lloyd-George: ibid., cols. 530–534.

32

December 13: Parliamentary Debates (Lords), 5th ser., 195
(1955):16–17.

33

Haden-Guest: ibid., cols. 58–59.

34

Teviot: ibid., col. 62.

34

Amulree: ibid., col. 83.

34

government decision: ibid., cols. 91–94. See also, throughout the
debate, *The Times,* "Parliamentary Report," 14 December
1955, p. 4; *Lancet* 1955 (2):1333–1335; these are more in-
formative about the temper of proceedings, and sometimes
more accurate about words actually said, since Hansard is
subject to silent emendation.

34

Brain Committee: The Interdepartmental Committee on Drug Addiction, Sir Russell Brain, chairman, was appointed on 3 June 1958. It issued an interim report on a couple of minor questions, and then: Great Britain, Ministry of Health, and Department of Health for Scotland, *Drug Addiction: Report of the Interdepartmental Committee,* 29 November 1960 (London: HMSO, 1961), hereafter cited as *Brain I.* The committee was reconvened in July 1964, and issued another report: Great Britain, Ministry of Health, and Scottish Home and Health Department, *Drug Addiction: The Second Report of the Interdepartmental Committee,* 31 July 1964 (London: HMSO, 1965), hereafter *Brain II.*

35

no cause to fear: Brain I, pp. 9, 11.

35

tribunals: ibid., p. 12.

35

specialized centers: ibid., p. 10.

35–36

Brain's talk: Sir Russell Brain, "The Report of the Interdepartmental Committee on Drug Addiction," ("Delivered before the Society for the Study of Addiction . . . [in] London on April 18th, 1961"), *British Journal of Addiction* 57 (1961):81–103 including discussion.

36

rise in addiction: Spear, "Growth of Heroin Addiction," tables, pp. 247–248.

36

Benjamin's objection: Brain's talk, "The Report . . . on Drug Addiction," discussion, pp. 92–93, 102; telephone interview with Irving Benjamin, London, January 1973.

36

reaction to Benjamin: Brain's talk, "The Report . . . on Drug Addiction," discussion, pp. 94, 101.

38

one consultant recalled: interview, Mitcheson, August 1972.

38

doubling every sixteen months: Thomas H. Bewley, Oved Ben-Arie, and I. Pierce James, "Morbidity and Mortality from Heroin Dependence, 1: Survey of Heroin Addicts Known to Home Office," *British Medical Journal* 1968 (1):726.

39–40

prescribing doctors: interviews, extensive; among others, Pierce James, Mitcheson, Chapple. *Brain II*, p. 6, asserts that "the evidence further shows that not more than six doctors have prescribed these very large amounts of dangerous drugs for individual patients . . ." and this figure has been repeated very widely, even by people who know there were more.

40

treatment centers shut down: interviews, Freedman, October 1973, Finney, July 1972.

41

Lady Frankau: details from several interview sources; *Brain II*, p. 6; I. M. Frankau and Patricia M. Stanwell, "The Treatment of Drug-Addiction," *Lancet* 1960 (2):1377.

42–43

good doctors: interviews, Home Office, August 1972; Chapple. John Hewetson and Robert Ollendorff, "Preliminary Survey of One Hundred London Heroin and Cocaine Addicts," *British Journal of Addiction* 60 (1964):109–114.

43–44

statistics and Table: Spear, "Growth of Heroin Addiction," tables, p.. 247–248.

45

scarcity of cannabis: Spear, "Growth of Heroin Addiction," pp. 249–251.

45–46

pill taking: Kenneth Leech, *Pastoral Care and the Drug Scene* (London: S.P.C.K., 1970), pp. 13–21.

46

blacks rare among addicts: interviews, Home Office, July and August 1972; Statistics and Research Division, Department of Health and Social Security, August 1972; Ian Pierce James, August 1972. I. Pierce James, "The Changing Pattern of Narcotic Addiction in Britain, 1959 to 1969," *International Journal of the Addictions* 6 (March 1971):124; Leech, *Pastoral Care and the Drug Scene,* pp. 29, 30.

46

drug use in Soho: ibid., p. 67.

47

drugs and social class, age, etc.: interviews, Home Office, Pierce James, Mitcheson. E. R. Bransby, "A Study of Patients Notified by Hospitals as Addicted to Drugs: First Report," *Health Trends* (London, Department of Health and Social Security) 3 (November 1971):75–78; G. V. Stimson, *Heroin and Behaviour* (Shannon: Irish University Press, 1973), pp. 66–70; Leech, *Pastoral Care and the Drug Scene,* p. 29.

48–49

addiction and crime: interviews, Commander Robert Huntley, New Scotland Yard, January 1973; Ian Pierce James, August 1972. I. Pierce James and P. T. D'Orbán, "Patterns of Delinquency among British Heroin Addicts," *Bulletin on Narcotics* 22 (April–June 1970):13–19, quotation from p. 19; I. Pierce James, "Delinquency and Heroin Addiction in Britain," *British Journal of Criminology* 9 (April 1969):108–124; Stimson, *Heroin and Behaviour,* pp. 74, 151–154.

49–51

Canadian addicts: interviews, Home Office, Zacune. H. B. Spear and M. M. Glatt, "The Influence of Canadian Addicts on Heroin Addiction in the United Kingdom," *British Journal of Addiction* 66 (1971):141–149; J. Zacune, "A Comparison of Canadian Narcotic Addicts in Great Britain and in Canada," *Bulletin on Narcotics* 23 (October–December 1971):41–49.

51

sick and dying: interviews, Thomas Bewley, August 1972 and (by telephone) December 1973. Bewley, Ben-Arie, and James, "Morbidity and Mortality," pp. 725, 726.

55

the coming consensus: Thomas Bewley, "Heroin and Cocaine Addiction," *Lancet* 1965 (1) (10 April):808–810.

56

doctors and patients: interview, Edwards, London, December 1973.

56

second report: Brain II, pp. 12, 7. See above, note to p. 34.

57

compulsory detention: Brain II, p. 9.

57

huddled through: for a highly personal account, see Kenneth Leech, *Keep the Faith Baby* (London: S.P.C.K., 1973), especially pp. 37–46.

57

1,290 addicts: Spear, "Growth of Heroin Addiction," p. 250, table 3.

58

Swan and Petro: details from various interviews, August 1972 and August 1973; from Margaret Tripp, August 1972; and others including youths who knew one or the other of them. Partial account in Leech, *Keep the Faith Baby,* pp. 42–46. And, for Swan, *The Times,* 14 June 1968, p. 3; 8 August 1968, p. 2; 22 July 1969, p. 2 (his application for a new trial); 25 February 1970, p. 2 (account of hearing before the General Medical Council). For Petro, *The Times,* 12 January 1968, p. 1; *Daily Mirror,* 12 January 1968, p. 1 (his arrest after Frost program); *The Times,* 1 June 1968, p. 1 (Petro to be struck off medical register); 27 June 1968, p. 3 (prescribing to addicts while awaiting appeal); 29 October 1968, p. 3.

59

fundamental aim of centers: Griffith Edwards, "Relevance of American Experience of Narcotic Addiction to the British Scene,"

British Medical Journal 1967 (3):425, 428. Edwards, "Drug Problems UK/USA," pp. 2, 5.

64

modification of long-term approach: e.g., leading article, *British Medical Journal* 1971 (2):321.

67

Lexington scales of abstinence: Lawrence Kolb and C. K. Himmelsbach, "Clinical Studies of Drug Addiction, III: A Critical Review of the Withdrawal Treatments with a Method for Evaluating Abstinence Syndromes," *American Journal of Psychiatry* 94 (January 1938):759–799; C. K. Himmelsbach, "The Morphine Abstinence Syndrome, Its Nature and Treatment," *Annals of Internal Medicine* 15 (October 1941):829–839.

67

fake withdrawal: interview, Connell, August 1972.

67–68

addicts' doses in England: interviews, Home Office, Tripp, Mitcheson, Pierce James, Oppenheim; dosage levels rechecked August 1973.

72–73

Philip Connell and withdrawal syndrome: interview, August 1972; rechecked with Dr. Connell, including the description of his research.

74

1700: John Jones, *The Mysteries of Opium Revealed* (London: Richard Smith, 1700), p. 20.

75–76

1968 experimental addiction: Ian Oswald, "Personal View," *British Medical Journal* 1969 (1) (February 15):438.

78

teens or twenties: Spear, "Growth of Heroin Addiction," tables, p. 248; Great Britain, Home Office Drugs Branch, "United Kingdom Statistics of Drug Addiction and Criminal Offences

Involving Drugs" (London: Home Office, yearly), 1973, sheets 1 and 3.

78

recent study: Herbert H. Blumberg, S. Daryl Cohen, B. Elizabeth Dronfield, Elizabeth A. Mordecai, J. Colin Roberts, David Hawks, "British Opiate Users: I. People Approaching London Drug Treatment Centres," *International Journal of the Addictions* 9 (1974):(in press).

78

multiple-drug use: ibid.

78

startling number: ibid.; David V. Hawks, "The Evaluation of Measures to Deal with Drug Dependence in the United Kingdom," in *Anglo-American Conference on Drug Abuse, Proceedings . . . 16–18 April 1973,* ed. R. A. Bowen (London: Royal Society of Medicine, 1973), p. 115; E. R. Bransby, Gail Curley, and Maryla Kotulanska, "A Study of Patients Notified by Hospitals as Addicted to Drugs: Second Report," *Health Trends* 5 (1973):17–20. Interviews, Roberts, Hawks.

80

pilot study: Douglas H. Powell, "A Pilot Study of Occasional Heroin Users," *Archives of General Psychology* 28:586–594.

81

availability of drugs: Blumberg, Cohen, Dronfield, Mordecai, Roberts, and Hawks, "British Opiate Users: I" (in press).

82

addiction seen differently: ibid.; N. H. Rathod, "The Use of Heroin and Methadone by Injection in a New Town," *British Journal of Addiction* 67 (1972):113–121; R. de Alarcón, "The Spread of Heroin Abuse in a Community," *Bulletin on Narcotics* 21 (July–September 1969):17–22; Adèle Kosviner, M. C. Mitcheson, Kenneth Myers, Alan Ogborne, G. V. Stimson, Jim Zacune, and Griffith Edwards, "Heroin Use in a Provincial Town," *Lancet* 1968 (1):1189–1192; Jim Zacune, Martin Mitcheson, and Sarah Malone, "Heroin Use in a Provincial

Town—One Year Later," *International Journal of the Addictions* 4 (December 1969):557–570.

82

differences and similarities in groups: Jock Young, *The Drugtakers: The Social Meaning of Drug Use* (London: MacGibbon and Kee, 1971); citation is to paperback ed. (London: Palladin, 1971), pp. 41–42, 47, 85–87; Jock Young, "Drug Use as Problem-Solving Behavior: A Subcultural Approach," *Anglo-American Conference on Drug Abuse, Proceedings . . . 16–18 April 1973,* ed. R. A. Bowen (London: Royal Society of Medicine, 1973), pp. 77–78. Interviews, Chapple, Bewley, Mitcheson, Tripp, Mack and Norvill.

82

Edwards: interview, December 1973.

83

Stimson and Ogborne: G. V. Stimson and A. C. Ogborne, "A Survey of a Representative Sample of Addicts Prescribed Heroin at London Clinics," *Bulletin on Narcotics* 22 (October–December 1970):13–22; Stimson, *Heroin and Behaviour,* especially the analysis and follow-up of the four types of addicts, pp. 130–206.

85

policies of clinic staffs: e.g., Herbert H. Blumberg, S. Daryl Cohen, B. Elizabeth Dronfield, Elizabeth A. Mordecai, J. Colin Roberts, and David Hawks, "British Opiate Users: II. Differences Between Those Given an Opiate Script and Those Not Given One," *International Journal of the Addictions* 9 (1974):205–220.

86

no central direction: interviews, Home Office and Department of Health and Social Security.

88

All Saints', Birmingham: interview, Edward David Hill, at the Birmingham clinic, August 1972. John Owens, "Centers for Treatment of Drug Addiction: Integrated Approach," *British Medical Journal* 1967 (2):501–502.

89

urinalyses: for the techniques available to the clinics at the time, D. J. Berry, J. Grove, B. Widdop, and J. H. P. Willis, "The Detection of Drugs of Dependence in Urine," *Bulletin on Narcotics* 22 (July–September 1970):31–37. Errors can occur: see J. G. Montalvo, C. B. Scrignar, E. Alderette, E. Harper, and D. Eyer, "Flushing, Pale-colored Urines, and False Negatives: Urinalysis of Narcotic Addicts," *International Journal of the Addictions* 7 (1972):355–364.

94–95

clinic staffing: interviews, Department of Health and Social Security, August, 1972; and with clinic directors previously noted, passim.

95

New York psychiatrists: telephone query to New York City branch office of American Psychiatric Association, June 1974.

95

New York doctors: New York State Board of Medical Examiners, computer printout of roster, 28 October 1973, provided to Medical Society of State of New York.

96–97

present clinic practices: interviews, as previously noted; observation at clinics at University College Hospital and Hackney Hospital, August and September 1972.

98

statistics: Home Office, "United Kingdom Statistics of Drug Addiction," 1973, sheets 1, 2, and 3.

99

ninety-eight who died: Thomas Bewley, unpublished research; interview with him, August 1972; the point rechecked with him, April 1974.

99

methylamphetamine epidemic: interviews, Home Office, Mitcheson, Tripp. I. Pierce James, "A Methylamphetamine Epidemic?"

letter to *Lancet* 1968 (1):916; Philip Connell, *Amphetamine Psychosis* (London: Oxford University Press, 1958), p. 129.

100

methylamphetamine and multiple-drug use: Martin Mitcheson, "Polydrug Abuse," *Community Health* 1969, reprinted in *ABC of Drug Addiction* (Bristol: John Wright and Sons, 1970), pp. 89–93; Martin Mitcheson, James Davidson, David Hawks, Laura Hitchens, and Sarah Malone, "Sedative Abuse by Heroin Addicts," *Lancet* 1970 (1):606–607; Leech, *Pastoral Care and the Drug Scene*, pp. 18–20, 67; Leech, *Keep the Faith Baby*, pp. 46–48; Margaret Tripp, "Who Speaks for Petro?" *Drugs and Society* 3 (November 1973):12–17. Interviews, Mitcheson, Connell, and Pierce James, August 1972.

101

"keep them alive": interview, James Willis.

101

pills in U.S.: interviews, Mitcheson, March 1973; Freedman, October 1973. Darryl S. Inaba, George R. Gay, John A. Newmeyer, and Craig Whitehead, "Methaqualone Abuse: 'Luding Out'," *Journal of the American Medical Association* 224 (11 June 1973):1505–1509; Emil F. Pascarelli, "Methaqualone Abuse, the Quiet Epidemic," *Journal of the American Medical Association* 224:1512.

102

lawful pills: B. M. Barraclough, "Are There Safer Hypnotics than Barbiturates?" *Lancet* 1974 (1) (12 January):57–58.

102–105

Chinese heroin: various interviews, August, September, December 1972, August 1973; interview, Huntley, New Scotland Yard, January 1973; interview, Aitken, December 1973.

104

convictions: Great Britain, Home Office, *Report to the United Nations by Her Majesty's Government . . . on the Working of the International Treaties on Narcotic Drugs* (London: Home Office, 1969), p. 13; ibid., 1972, p. 10.

105–106

statistics: Home Office, "United Kingdom Statistics of Drug Addiction," 1973, sheets 1 and 2; Great Britain, Department of Health and Social Security, *Annual Report* (London: HMSO), 1969, pp. 283–284; 1970, p. 299.

105

pessimistic calculation: Hawks, "Evaluation of Measures to Deal with Drug Dependence," p. 115.

108

addicts' complaints: interviews with addicts, and with Don Aitken.

108

discovery of methadone: Ervin C. Kleiderer, Justus B. Rice, Victor Conquest, and James H. Williams, *Pharmaceutical Activities at the I. G. Farbenindustrie Plant, Höchst am Main,* report PB-981 (Washington: Department of Commerce, Office of the Publication Board, July 1945), pp. 85–86.

109

methadone blockade: Vincent P. Dole and Marie Nyswander, "A Medical Treatment for Diacetylmorphine (Heroin) Addiction," *Journal of the American Medical Association* 139 (1965): 81–82, 83.

109–110

criticisms of methadone: interviews, Congressman Charles Rangel; Dr. James Wesley, director of drug programs, Harlem Hospital; Graham Finney, June and July 1972. Florence Heyman, "Methadone Maintenance as Law and Order," *Society,* June 1972, pp. 15–25. James Williams, "The Methadone Debate," *Drugs and Society* 2 (January 1973):17–18; James M. Markham, "Methadone Therapy Programs: Issue and Debate," *New York Times,* 17 April 1973, p. 30; Henry J. Lennard, Leon J. Epstein, and Mitchell S. Rosenthal, "The Methadone Illusion," *Science* 176 (26 May 1972):881–884, and the ensuing correspondence, idem, 179 (16 March 1973), including authors' reply, pp. 1078–1079; R. J. Bozell, "Drug Abuse: Methadone Becomes the Solution and the Problem," *Science* 179:772–775.

110–112

methadone in England: interviews with clinic directors generally, as previously cited, and particularly with Mitcheson, Mack, Bewley, Tripp, Oppenheim, August 1972.

112

442 on heroin alone: Home Office, "United Kingdom Statistics of Drug Addiction," 1973, sheet 2 (by computation from data there).

112

amounts prescribed: data from Institute for the Study of Drug Dependence, London, August 1972 and April 1974, and elsewhere.

112

tribunals: under regulations issued by the Home Office pursuant to the *Misuse of Drugs Act, 1971* (London: HMSO, 1971), Sec. 16, Sched. 3, Pt. I.

115

civil servant from New York: interview, Finney.

115–117

"costing the clinics": letter with costs from Department of Health and Social Security, 19 October 1972.

119

addicts getting older: Home Office, *Report to the United Nations . . . on Narcotic Drugs,* 1968–1972, comparing statistical table at para. 34.

124

Mitcheson: interview, March 1973, and conversations since.

125

billion dollars: United States, National Commission on Marihuana and Drug Abuse, *Drug Use in America: Problem in Perspective,* Second Report of the National Commission . . . (Washington, D.C.: Government Printing Office, March 1973), p. 3.

125

"drug abuse industrial complex": loc. cit.

126

Vera Institute: full citations at note to p. 11, above.

127

grandiose scheme: Vera Institute of Justice, staff memorandum, "The Use of Dangerous Drugs in the United States and England," 12 November 1966.

127

10,000 addicts: ibid., p. 9.

127

thinking of Home Office: Charles G. Jeffery, "Drug Control in the U.K.," in *Modern Trends in Drug Dependence and Alcoholism,* ed. R. V. Phillipson (London: Butterworth, 1970), p. 67. Despite publication date, Jeffery's text makes clear it was written before the British clinics were functioning.

127

credited British clinics: Charles Lidz, "The British Experience with Heroin and Other Opiates," Appendix C in Riordan and Gould, *Vera Institute Proposal,* p. C-6.

127

therapeutic communities: interviews, Freedman, Zinberg, October 1973. Markham, "What's All This Talk of Heroin Maintenance," p. 7; John C. Kramer, "The Evaluation of Measures to Deal with Drug Dependence in the U.S.A.," *Anglo-American Conference on Drug Abuse, Proceedings . . . 16–18 April, 1973,* ed. R. A. Bowen (London: Royal Society of Medicine, 1973), pp. 110, 111.

127–128

methadone numbers and problems: Koran, "Heroin Maintenance for Heroin Addicts," p. 655; also see citations at pp. 109–110, above.

128

quarantine: Steven Jonas, "Heroin Utilization: A Communicable Disease?" *New York State Journal of Medicine* 72 (1972): 1292; idem, letter to editor, *New England Journal of Medicine* 288 (22 February 1973):421–422; "Quarantining of

Drug Addicts Urged to Halt Epidemics," *New York Times*, 8 May 1972, p. 74; ibid., 12 April 1972, p. 30.

128

considered with interest: "Proposal to Supply Free Heroin to Addicts Is Vigorously Condemned by Harlem Groups and Individuals," *New York Times*, 9 April 1972, p. 31.

128

Washington: American Bar Association, Special Committee on Crime Prevention and Control, *New Perspectives in Urban Crime* (Washington, D.C.: American Bar Association, 1972), p. 62.

128

impulsive legislator, Samuels: Markham, "What's All This Talk of Heroin Maintenance," p. 8.

129

the plan itself: Riordan and Gould, *Vera Institute Proposal*, pp. 3–4, 6–7.

129

"drug of choice": ibid., p. 5.

130

clinic procedures: ibid., pp. 14–16.

130

pilot-group assessment: ibid., pp. 17–18.

130

larger study: ibid., pp. 19 et seq.

131

Rangel: U.S. Congress, House, *Congressional Record* (Extensions of Remarks), 18 February 1972, p. E 1358.

131

Ingersoll: speech to California Peace Officers Association, 24 May 1972.

132

Peyser's bills: H.R. 16458, *Congressional Record,* 17 August 1972, p. H. 7870; H.R. 16617, *Congressional Record,* 12 September 1972, p. H. 8299; cited in Koran, "Heroin Maintenance for Heroin Addicts," p. 656.

132

Dole: Vincent P. Dole, editorial, *Journal of the American Medical Association* 220 (12 June 1972):1493.

132–133

Densen-Gerber: Markham, "What's All This Talk of Heroin Maintenance," p. 30.

133

Bejerot: ibid., p. 30.

133

B.N.D.D. study: William H. McGlothlin, Victor A. Tabbush, Carl D. Chambers, and Kay Jamison, *Alternative Approaches to Opiate Addiction Control: Costs, Benefits, and Potential* (Washington: U.S. Department of Justice, Bureau of Narcotics and Dangerous Drugs, June 1972), pp. 1, 3–4.

133

civil commitment: ibid., p. 45 et seq.

134

courts slow: ibid., p. 46.

134

addict thefts: ibid., Appendix A, p. A4.

134

Rockefeller estimate: Drug Abuse Council, *A Perspective on "Get Tough" Drug Laws* (Washington: Drug Abuse Council, Inc., May 1973), p. 3.

134

F.B.I. estimate: United States, Department of Justice, Federal Bureau of Investigation, *Uniform Crime Reports* (Washington, D.C.: Government Printing Office, annually), 1970, pp. 18–28; 1971, pp. 15–29; 1972, pp. 15–28.

134–135
McGlothlin's total costs: McGlothlin et al., *Alternative Approaches,*
      Appendix A, pp. A2, A8.

135
McGlothlin on British "system": ibid., pp. 31, 33.

136
reduction in thefts: ibid., p. 36.

136
foregone production: ibid., pp. A18–A19.

136–137
large majority committed: ibid., p. 45.

138
doctors disgusted: interview, Newman, June 1972.

139
greatest fear: Lewis, "A Heroin Maintenance Program in the U.S.?"
      p. 546.

140
U.S. National Commission: U.S. National Commission on Marihuana
      and Drug Abuse, *Drug Use in America,* pp. 334, 373.

140
advocates: for review of these arguments, Koran, "Heroin Main-
      tenance for Heroin Addicts," pp. 654–656, 660; Brecher and
      editors of Consumer Reports, *Licit and Illicit Drugs,* pp. 134,
      530.

143
no more bad trips: the climbing but changed pattern of use of LSD
      is widely reported; it was confirmed in interviews, for exam-
      ple, with Freedman and Blum, September and October 1973.

145–146
Edwards: interview, December 1973.

155–156
statistics: see pages 158–160.

Index